New and Delightful Juvenile.

SPECTACLES FOR LITTLE EYES.

A very attractive volume, 16mo. With forty illustrations on wood. 60 cents.

THE CHURCH OF THE FIRST THREE CENTURIES.

OR,

Notices of the Lives and Opinions of some of the Early Fathers, with special reference to the Doctrine of the Trinity; illustrating its late Origin and gradual Formation.

By ALVAN LAMSON, D. D.

8vo. $1.75.

"In this erudite work, an exposition is given of the early theology of the Christian Church, as exemplified in the opinions of Justin Martyr, Clement of Alexandria, Origen, and Eusebius." — *New York Tribune.*

"Dr. Lamson's careful habits of inquiry, sagacious discernment, candid moderation, familiarity with ancient learning, and lucid and direct style, have produced a work full of entertaining information, which can be depended upon for its accuracy, and attractive by its literary execution." — *Christian Register.*

"We conceive this to be a highly valuable publication. It shows the human origin of the doctrine of the Trinity, and traces its gradual growth, and incorporation into the Christian Church." — *Christian Ambassador.*

"Dr. Lamson has given to his subject an investigation searching and thorough: he has brought to its treatment a learning and study seldom surpassed by any late theological writer, and a mind capable of arriving at views of judicial calmness, and freedom from prejudice." — *Norfolk Co. Journal.*

"A work like this, from so excellent a theologian and scholar as Dr. Lamson, will be highly acceptable to persons who desire 'to know of the doctrine' which it is intended to illustrate." — *Boston Advertiser.*

WOMAN'S RIGHTS UNDER THE LAW.

THREE LECTURES DELIVERED IN BOSTON, JANUARY, 1861.

By MRS. C. H. DALL,

Author of "Woman's Right to Labor," "Historical Pictures Retouched," &c.

16mo. Cloth, 63 cts.

Lecture 1. The Oriental Estimate, and the French Law.
" 2. The English Common Law.
" 3. The United States Law, and some Thoughts on Human Rights.

TRACTS FOR PRIESTS AND PEOPLE.

A Series of Papers,

By HUGHES (Author of "Tom Brown"), PROF. MAURICE, and other eminent Churchmen, responsive to the world-famous "Essays and Reviews" ("Recent Inquiries in Theology").

12mo. $1.00.

Christ in the Will, the Heart, and the Life. By Rev. A. B. MUZZEY. 12mo. $1.00.

"A very readable and acceptable addition to our library of practical religion." — *Christian Examiner.*

"These Discourses were written and preached at various periods of their author's ministry, and are dedicated to his parishioners. They embrace a large range of subjects, all of which are treated with the force and eloquence which are well-known characteristics of their eminent author." — *Boston Traveller.*

Hymns for Mothers and Children. Selected and edited by one of the compilers of "Hymns of the Ages." Printed on delicately tinted paper, and adorned by an appropriate title-page and frontispiece, and six exquisite vignettes by Billings. Second Edition. Square 16mo. $1.25.

"There is not a commonplace or an inferior piece in the whole selection: a beautiful design, carried out with excellent judgment and taste, and consummated with the daintiest skill of printer, engraver, and binder." — *N. Y. Independent.*

"Full of rare gems of song and verse, which give beautiful expression to many of the holiest feelings which can fill the heart." — *New-Englander.*

Struggle for Life. By the Author of several brilliant papers in the Atlantic Monthly, — "The Queen of the Red Chess-men," "Sunshine," and others. 12mo. $1.00.

Kormak: an Icelandic Romance of the Tenth Century. In Six Cantos. 16mo. 75 cents.

"A romance unique, instructive, and interesting. Opening the book at the title-page, we could not leave it till we had read to the closing line." — *Gospel Banner.*

In Press.

ALTAR AT HOME. Second Series.

With choice Selections, and Original Prayers, from about twenty-five eminent clergymen.

Recent Inquiries in Theology.

("*Essays and Reviews.*")

BY ENGLISH CHURCHMEN.

Edited, with an Introduction, by Rev. F. H. HEDGE, D.D.

THE EDUCATION OF THE WORLD. By Frederick Temple, D. D., Chaplain in Ordinary to the Queen, Head Master of Rugby.
BUNSEN'S BIBLICAL RESEARCHES. By Rowland Williams, D. D.
ON THE STUDY OF THE EVIDENCES OF CHRISTIANITY. By Baden Powell.
SEANCES HISTORIQUES DE GENEVE. THE NATIONAL CHURCH. By Henry Bristow Wilson, B. D.
ON THE MOSAIC COSMOGONY. By C. W Goodwin, M. A.
TENDENCIES OF RELIGIOUS THOUGHT IN ENGLAND. By Mark Pattison, B. D.
ON THE INTERPRETATION OF SCRIPTURE. By Benjamin Jowett, M. A.
NOTE ON BUNSEN'S BIBLICAL RESEARCHES.

In one vol. 12mo. $1.25.

☞ The unprecedented stir made in England by this remarkable publication, which has been followed by a commotion in this country but little inferior to that produced abroad, renders any extended notice of the volume, or parade of editorial notices, superfluous.

The English sale has already reached *twenty thousand copies*, and continues unabated. In this country several large editions have been exhausted, notwithstanding the times; and the interest is increasing. No thoughtful man will wish to be without so marked and important a volume.

French "ESSAYS AND REVIEWS."

THE PROGRESS OF RELIGIOUS THOUGHT AS ILLUSTRATED IN THE PROTESTANT CHURCH OF FRANCE;

Being Essays and Reviews, bearing on the Chief Religious Questions of the Day. Translated from the French; with an Introductory Essay on the "Oxford Essays and Reviews," by the Editor, JOHN R. BEARD, D. D. Post 8vo, $1.75.

THE TRUE STORY

OF

THE BARONS OF THE SOUTH;

OR,

THE RATIONALE OF THE AMERICAN CONFLICT.

BY E. W. REYNOLDS,

AUTHOR OF "THE RECORDS OF BUBBLETON PARISH," ETC., ETC.

"All our misfortunes arise from a single source, the resistance of the Southern Colonies to Republican Government. . . . . Popular principles and axioms are abhorrent to the inclinations of the Barons of the South." — JOHN ADAMS *in* 1776.

BOSTON:
WALKER, WISE, AND COMPANY,
245 WASHINGTON STREET.
1862.

CAMBRIDGE:
WELCH, BIGELOW, AND COMPANY,
PRINTERS TO THE UNIVERSITY.

TO

THE JUST MEN AND WOMEN OF MY COUNTRY,

WHO,

LOYAL TO LIBERTY IN ITS DARKEST HOUR,

HAVE SOUGHT THE TRUE GLORY OF THE REPUBLIC, BY VINDICATING THE RIGHTS OF HUMANITY IN THE PERSONS OF THE LOWLIEST IN THE LAND;

AND WHO SEE,

BEYOND THE CARNIVAL OF BATTLE,

A RACE REDEEMED, AND A NATION RENOVATED,

I inscribe this Essay,

WITH GRATEFUL REMEMBRANCE OF THEIR SERVICES, AND PROFOUND RESPECT FOR THEIR VIRTUES.

"'A NEGRO has a *soul*, an' please your honor,' said the Corporal (*doubtingly*).

"'I am not much versed, Corporal,' quoth my Uncle Toby, 'in things of that kind; but I suppose God would not leave him without one any more than thee or me.'

"'It would be putting one sadly over the head of the other,' quoth the Corporal.

"'It would so,' said my Uncle Toby.

"'Why, then, an' please your honor, is a black man to be used worse than a white one?'

"'I can give no reason,' said my Uncle Toby.

"'Only,' cried the Corporal, shaking his head, 'because he has no one to stand up for him.'

"'It is that very thing, Trim,' quoth my Uncle Toby, 'which recommends him to protection.'" — STERNE.

"We must not allow negroes to be MEN, lest we ourselves should be suspected of not being CHRISTIANS." — MONTESQUIEU.

"The man is thought a knave or fool,
  Or bigot, plotting crime,
Who, for the advancement of his kind,
  Is wiser than his time.
For him the hemlock shall distil;
  For him the axe be bared;
For him the gibbet shall be built;
  For him the stake prepared;
Him shall the scorn and wrath of men
  Pursue with deadly aim;
And malice, envy, spite, and lies
  Shall desecrate his name.
But truth shall conquer at the last;
  For round and round we run,
And ever the right comes uppermost,
  And ever is justice done."

MACKAY.

INTRODUCTION.

By Rev. SAMUEL J. MAY.

Oil and water cannot be made to unite, unless you first destroy their distinctive qualities, that is, make them something else than oil and water. Light and darkness cannot come together in the same enclosure, no, not on the same hemisphere, without modifying each other. Much less can liberty and slavery abide at peace in the same country, nor, indeed, on the same continent. They are, like good and evil, Christ and Belial, natural, eternal antagonists, utterly irreconcilable, mutually destructive.

The founders of our Republic reluctantly consented that the impracticable experiment should be attempted. And the disastrous consequences of that attempt have come upon this generation.

Could the framers of our Constitution have foreseen what our eyes behold, they would never have consented to any compromises with slave-holders, expressed or implied. Rather than permit our nation ever to become what it has been for the last thirty years, they would have deferred indefinitely its establishment, if that had been the alternative. If this Union could not have been formed without their agreeing that the Federal Government should erelong be put into the hands of a slave-holding oligarchy, to be wielded especially for the maintenance and extension of their system of oppression, our political fathers would have said, 'Then let it pass, — the object of our fondest hope, our longing desire! Much as we have suffered, much as we have sacrificed, we had rather abandon our great enterprise, and return even to the subjection from which we have just fought our way out, than to impose a worse bondage upon others. Better will it be, more safe, more honorable, to be ourselves again the subjects of a king, than to become the tyrant-masters of any of our fellow-men, or the accomplices of such despots.' But the wise and good men of 1787 did not foresee, nor apprehend, the catastrophe which their descendants of the second and third generations would witness. They did not foresee nor apprehend, that the government they instituted with so much care, in so much wisdom (save only in one covert point), would so soon be converted into a conspiracy against the natural and inalienable rights of man, "a mere plot for the extension and perpetuation of slavery" of the worst type; and that the "Barons of the South," whom they conciliated by their concessions, would attempt the dissolution of the Union, would involve these United States in all the horrors of civil war, rather than submit to those who only insisted upon conducting the general government on the principles and in the spirit of the Constitution.

Far otherwise: they confidently trusted that the love of freedom, which had inspired the American Colonies to attempt their deliverance from a foreign yoke, and had sustained them through a long, unequal conflict with the mightiest power on earth, was so rife everywhere, South as well as North, that in due time it would expel from every State every vestige of oppression.

In this belief the friends of liberty were encouraged by the abolition of slavery in all the States north of the Potomac; the frequency of private manumissions in the Southern States; and the unanimity with which the members of Congress, in 1807, concurred in an Act to suppress forever the African slave-trade, and punish as pirates all who should thereafter be found engaged in it. Thenceforward, for more than a decade of years, the philanthropists of the country, the Abolitionists, rested from their labors, in the belief that a spirit was abroad in the land which would accomplish the desire of their hearts, the deliverance of the enslaved. It was not until 1820, when the question of the admission of Missouri as a slave State, in violation of the Ordinance of 1787, agitated the country, that the people of the Northern States waked up to notice the "inclinations of the Barons of the South," and to mark the encroachments they had quietly but persistently made during the foregoing ten years.

Since that time, the strife between the friends of freedom and the abettors of slavery has waxed stronger and hotter, until now our whole country is involved in a most deadly civil war, which can never terminate until the cause of it, slavery, is removed.

For more than thirty years the Abolitionists have been endeavoring to rouse the people to exterminate "the evil thing" from our midst by moral, ecclesiastical, and political instrumentalities; urging them to their duty by the solemn admonition of the great prophet of our Revolution, that, "if they would not liberate the slaves by the generous energies of mind and heart, they would be liberated by the awful processes of civil and servile war." But the counsels of the Abolitionists have been spurned, their sentiments and purposes shamelessly misrepresented, their characters traduced, and their persons maltreated. And lo! now our beloved country, favored of Heaven above all others, is given up to fratricidal, parricidal, it may be suicidal war.

That the "Barons of the South" and their retainers have long been preparing for this diabolical rebellion, and have intended to be utterly unscrupulous as to the means they should use to effect their purpose, is daily becoming more patent. Their dark secrets are being brought to light. Every day new revelations are made of their impious, infernal plot. Evidences of their malice long prepense are continually coming from unexpected quarters. Inquiring eyes have discovered proofs of their guilt as black and damning as that of "the rebel angels."

The modest author of the following book has been impelled to come forth from his loved retirement, as a witness against them. It has been our privilege to hear, from the manuscript, the greater part of what he now offers to the public. We have advised the publication of it, because, though much to the same effect has been given in sundry speeches and newspaper articles, we have seen nothing so thorough, so radical. He has indeed gone to the root of the matter.

Everything in this book is racy, evidently the result of the author's own investigations; the product of his own thought. Some parts of it are wholly original. The reader will find in it a few facts more startling than any other explorer has brought us from the arcana of American despotism. He has shown us again, that "the children of this world have been wiser in their day and generation than the children of light." He has shown us that "the Barons of the South," as the illustrious John Adams first called them in 1776, have, almost from the beginning, hated democratic principles and purposes. They have foreseen and forefelt the utter incompatibility of a democratic government with the permanence of their "peculiar institution," — that worst system of tyranny, — and therefore they early determined to rule or to ruin the Republic; to change its character; to make it a ruthless despotism under a better name; or else to break away from it, rend it in twain, tear it in pieces. All this is made to appear on the following pages. We earnestly commend them to the attentive perusal of every one who is willing to know how implacable is the temper, how impious the purpose, of the leaders of this great Rebellion.

SYRACUSE, *January* 15, 1862.

CONTENTS.

PART I.

OUR TWO SYSTEMS OF SOCIETY.

PART II.

OUR POLITICAL APOSTASY.

PART III.

OUR POLITICAL REGENERATION.

PART IV.

THE REBELLION OF THE BARONS.

PART V.

THE PROVIDENTIAL ALTERNATIVE.

PART I.

OUR TWO SYSTEMS OF SOCIETY.

"IT cannot be denied that in a community spreading over a large extent of territory, and politically founded upon the principles proclaimed in the Declaration of Independence, but differing so widely in the elements of their social condition, that the inhabitants of one half the territory are wholly free, and those of the other half divided into masters and slaves, DEEP if not IRRECONCILABLE COLLISIONS OF INTEREST must abound. The question WHETHER SUCH A COMMUNITY CAN EXIST UNDER ONE COMMON GOVERNMENT, is a subject of profound philosophical speculation in theory. Whether it can continue long to exist, is a question to be solved only by the experiment now making by the people of this Union, under that national compact, the Constitution of the United States." — JOHN QUINCY ADAMS, 1833.

"The whole politics of rival States consist in checking the growth of one another." — MACHIAVEL.

"Hardly had the country recovered from its external struggles and internal troubles, than the most eminent and sagacious of the American statesmen became apprehensive as to the nature of the disease with which they had inoculated the national being; and fears as to the dangers which might be evolved out of the perpetuation of slavery were openly and solemnly expressed. Gradually it became apparent that, however highly the Slave States prized republican institutions, they prized slavery more, — that slavery, instead of dwindling away, was establishing itself permanently as a commercial as well as a social institution, and allying itself with political power, — that it was creating out of the Union a 'North' and a 'South,' — and that the necessity for its extension into new territory would cause a perpetual and ever-increasing antagonism between them, with an ever-growing divergence of feeling and interest. . . . . . America has thus reached a position in which the two sections are as far asunder in opinion as they can be; they are, in fact, diametrically opposed in respect to the fundamental ideas on which social and political institutions are based." — NORTH BRITISH REVIEW, 1861.

I.

NATURE OF THE CONFLICT.

WE trust that it has become obvious, by this time, to all the spectators as well as participants of the pending struggle, that the American Civil War is not a mere flash of sectional petulance, wantonly provoked by unnecessary aggressions, — the work of a few fanatical Abolitionists, on one side, and of desperate demagogues, on the other, — but a war of Principles, — a war of historical forces, lying deep as the foundations of human nature, and working wide as the scope of human action.

This being the real fact, we trust it is fast becoming equally obvious that there can be no "compromise" between the hostile powers, and no permanent, immediate, or desirable peace; — that, in a word, there can be no settlement of the great quesion at issue, which would be either honorable or profitable, except on the complete subjugation of the criminal party, and the complete extinction of that infamous system which — never compatible with political purity — is no longer compatible with the liberties or safety of the land.

It has been well observed, that "The slave question in America is only one phase of the more comprehensive question of human freedom that now begins to agitate the civilized world, and that presents the grand problem of the present age. Such a question must be met, must be discussed, must be decided, and decided correctly, before the nations of the earth can be enfranchised, and before this anomalous republic can either secure her own liberties or find permanent repose. In a nation whose declaration of self-evident and inalienable human rights has been hailed as the watchword for a universal struggle against despotic governments, — a nation whose support of human chattelhood has armed the world's despots with their most plausible pleas against republican institutions, it is in vain to expect that the discussion of such incongruities can be smothered, or the adjustment of them much longer postponed." *

All great nations have been called to face great perils, to exhibit great virtues, and to achieve great victories. The proof and seal of their greatness has been, that they have been strong in the day of calamity, generous and bold to meet the requirements of the hour, and have woven the scarlet threads of war into robes of immortal honor. What other people have been called

* William Goodell.

to face, to endure, and to suffer, in the formation of a strong nationality, may reasonably be exacted of us; and we are authorized in believing that the RESULT which God has in view will justify and reward the sacrifices involved in the contest.

What is it, for instance, that has formed the sterling qualities of the English nation, — the vigor, persistence, patience, enterprise, and heroism that distinguish the national character? These qualities are the product of the roughest discipline that ever spun the fibres of political greatness. They are the result of a providential collision and blending of races, under the impetus of conquest, under the hammer of affliction. The Briton and the Dane, the Saxon and the Norman, were thrust into the furnace in the historic process, and welded into an empire in the white heat of battle. War was the instrument, blood cemented the rising edifice, but the English monarchy is the solid result.

There are respects in which the present war will redound to the greatness of this country, aside from the attainment of the special objects for which it is waged. It will bring out the latent energy of our people; it will prove their loyalty, their fertility of resource, their self-denial; it will school them in patience and fortitude, and show the world what ardent patriotism has flowed in our calmer blood, and what power has slumbered, unseen, through the peaceful summer of our history. It will teach us all that there are better things to live for than riches and pride, or houses and lands, and permit us to lavish on the precious institutions and imperilled interests of our country the money and labor that would have been wasted on vanity and ambition. It will enable millions of us, who might have lived common lives, — who might have sauntered through the world aimless and imbecile, — who might have fatted and died like the cattle, but for this great peril of liberty and the salutary spur of a stern necessity, — it will enable these to enroll themselves among the benefactors of mankind, and to file into the illustrious ranks of patriots and heroes. It will *transfigure* our tame and prosaic life into the poetic colors that all memorable ages wear, and admit us to the solemn fellowship of the great dead, who have made the earth a battle-ground for righteousness, and twisted its harvests of thorns into chaplets for heaven.

It is these experiences that ennoble a nation. They break the enervating enchantment of luxurious living, and fire and purify the land with moral enthusiasm. Whatever may be the evils involved in such a conflict, — and they are neither few nor trivial, — the eventual blessings transcend them. Men cease to be triflers and hypocrites before the apparition of a great catastrophe. The good and evil qualities of men declare themselves in a vital social crisis. Every man, detached from his conventional anchorage, seeks his affinity. The moral nature comes uppermost, and life assumes a higher significance as sensuous superfluities become stripped away and we hear the voice of God in thunders that rock the temple of Liberty to its base.

It is our fortune to live in what will doubtless be esteemed, in after times, the most memorable epoch of our country's history. We have not been called into existence to share a torpid land, or to fulfil vacant years. God bids us live in the central current of his providence, and permits us to be servants and witnesses of his unfolding kingdom. He plants us on the ramparts of liberty, to guard the fairest heritage of humanity. He stations us at the wheel of the great constitutional ship, to pilot her through the stormy straits. He calls us to bear the battle's brunt, and take a trophy worthy of the momentous day.

Dwelling here on this latest scene of historic interest, amid the springs of ever-gushing events, how deep and full is the life of every loyal man! In the circuit of a single year — while the trumpet of battle is sounding, and we are bringing our holiest sacrifices to the altar of our country — we imbibe a more vital existence than we had ever tasted. We taste the emotions that swept through the souls of our fathers when they pledged life, fortune, and sacred honor to the cause of Freedom; the emotions that exalted LUTHER before his regal judges, that guided MILTON's pen to coin undying words, that followed SIDNEY to the block; and, like them, we are permitted to feel that this world has no joys which we cannot resign for the sake of a loyal conscience, an intrepid will, and a mind superior to fate. Like the noblest men who have dignified past ages, some of us are now permitted to realize how God makes the world a crucible for the refining of nations; — how he rescues the precious stones and the gold of every civilization, while he burns the dross in renovating fire; how he preserves every spiritual treasure, but shakes down our idols with remorseless austerity; and how, with unerring skill, he prunes our luxurious life, and saves only the branches that bear fruit for God and man.

II.

THE GERM OF THE CONFLICT.—THE BARONS ESPOUSE SLAVERY.

THE germ of the momentous contest in which the nation is now engaged is to be sought as far back as the beginning of our history. When, in the eventful year 1620, the ocean bore on its turbulent bosom a band of Puritans to Massachusetts and a cargo of negroes to Virginia, it deposited on our soil two hostile elements,—the seeds of two rival social systems,—the story of whose growth and expansion, of whose competitions and aggressions, forms the distinctive history of the Republic, down to this day.

The May-Flower brought the germ of a civilization in which thought is free,—learning diffused like the light,—law made the equal bulwark of every individual,—labor compensated and honored;—a civilization in which the rights of every man are recognized, the prerogatives of every class and sect protected, and the largest development of the whole body of society encouraged.

The Dutch ship brought, with its menial cargo, the germ of a social order radically different,—a social order that regards the State as existing solely for the benefit of a dominant class, which it arms accordingly with absolute and irresponsible power, and to which the other members of the community are related as cattle are related to their owners, — a social order in which justice is ignored, learning restricted, genius and enterprise discouraged, labor extorted and dishonored, the dictates of religion contemned, all improvement vetoed, and the organic forces that are intended to develop and magnify a state stricken with deadly paralysis.

It should have been morally self-evident, in the beginning, that these two social orders could never mature — within the same national domain — without coming into collision, shocking the government to its centre, and involving the destruction of at least one of the antagonistic interests. The event was inevitable as the working of instincts in the blood, its fulfilment only a question of time.

The antithesis has a yet deeper root. The Puritans who came to Massachusetts left a sturdy brotherhood in England, who overturned the throne of Charles I., reared a Commonwealth out of the chaos of civil war, and engendered among the English people a republican spirit, that allowed the kingdom no rest till bounds were set to the royal prerogative, and the rights of the subject fortified by law. The Cavaliers who settled in Virginia — assuming the charge of that peculiar "property" brought over by the Dutch slave-trader — were of that effeminate and supercilious nobility * that drew the lance in behalf of the oppressive Stuarts; that poured out treasure and life so profusely in defence of a family whose crafty malice was equalled only by its scandalous vices and impotent imbecility; and that resisted with such virulent hostility the spirit of political reform marshalled under Cromwell and William of Orange.

Thus the two parties — the representatives of liberty and oppression — whose struggles comprise the glory and shame of English history in the seventeenth century, delegated their quarrel to the new empire then rising in the West; and here, accordingly, under modified conditions, we are fighting to reach an issue far grander and more momentous than that which banished James II. and gave a new dynasty to England.

* Respecting the first emigrants to Virginia, I find the following statements, copied from Willson's American History: — "Of the one hundred and five persons on the list of emigrants destined to remain, there were no men with families, — there were but twelve laborers, and very few mechanics. The rest were composed of gentlemen of fortune, and of persons of no occupation, — mostly of idle and dissolute habits, — who had been tempted to join the expedition through curiosity or the hope of gain; a company but poorly calculated to plant an agricultural state in a wilderness." (p. 162.) "New emigrants arrived in 1609, most of whom were profligate and disorderly persons, who had been sent off to escape a worse destiny at home." (p. 166.) At the time of the first importation of negroes (1620), "there were very few women in the Colony." "Ninety women of reputable character" were soon after sent over, and the colonists purchased them for wives, "the price of a wife rising from one hundred and twenty to one hundred and fifty pounds of tobacco." (p. 170.) Is this the origin, after all, of the celebrated First Families of Virginia?

The two antagonistic systems found congenial soil in the places where they were planted. Freedom was cherished in Massachusetts, slavery was fostered in Virginia. There was a momentary effort, it is true, to establish an aristocracy in the Puritan Colony; but it was found hostile to the temper of the province. It is true, also, that slavery obtained a temporary footing in this Colony, as in all the other Colonies, and that the slave-trade formed an important part of the early commerce of New England. But it was impossible that the system should long survive, in opposition to that intense love of freedom which was the salt of the otherwise unsavory character of the Puritans, and in the face of the institutions they founded and matured. To Massachusetts belongs the honor of having been the first of the States to abolish negro slavery by a solemn judicial decision. In Virginia, the baleful plant of despotism became rooted deeper in her growing polity in the process of time. In the first instance, negroes were enslaved on the ground that they were heathen; but as they began to be converted and Christianized, it became necessary to base their servitude on their alleged inferiority as a race. Having thus subverted the liberties of the negroes, the Virginia planters proceeded to curtail the rights of the other race, and poor white men were disfranchised by an act of the Provincial Assembly.*

* Hildreth's History of the United States, Vol. I. pp. 523, 524.

The political tendencies of the two Colonies were consistent with their antecedents. On the breaking out of the English civil war, Massachusetts indicated her sympathies by dropping the oath of allegiance and furling for a while the red cross of England, while Virginia, with Maryland, adhered to the king, and piously cursed the Roundheads who were prevailing against him.*

The same distinction is observable with respect to social improvement. As early as 1649, the freemen of Massachusetts — "in order that learning may not be buried in the grave of our fathers" — enacted that every township should maintain a school for reading and writing, and every town of a hundred householders a grammar school, with a teacher qualified "to fit youths for the University." This school law was adopted by the sister Colonies of New England, — that of Rhode Island alone excepted.† But in Virginia, as late as 1671, Governor Berkeley said, — in a Report made to the Privy Council, — "I thank God there are no free schools nor printing, and I hope we shall not have these hundred years; for learning has brought disobedience and heresy and sects into the world, and printing has divulged them, and libels against the best government: God keep us from both!"‡

* Hildreth's History, Vol. I. pp. 285, 339.

† Ibid., pp. 370, 371.

‡ Ibid., p. 526.

The extreme pertinacity with which the Southern Colonies adhered to the slave system is well illustrated in the early history of Georgia. General James Oglethorpe — a member of the British Parliament, and a man whose enlightened views and humane policy render him worthy of an honorable remembrance — "conceived the idea of opening for the poor of his own country, and for the persecuted Protestants of all nations, an asylum in America." In 1733, having obtained a grant from the king, he landed at Savannah with one hundred and twenty immigrants, and commenced a settlement. In this infant society, slavery was strictly prohibited, and pronounced, "not only immoral, but contrary to the laws of England."

But, unfortunately for this attempt to plant a free state, most of the first emigrants were not accustomed to labor. "The Colony did not prosper," and the colonists began to complain that they were prohibited the use of slave labor. "The regulations of the trustees began to be evaded, and the laws against slavery were not rigidly enforced. At first, slaves from South Carolina were hired for short periods; then for a hundred years, or during life; and a sum equal to the value of the negro paid in advance." In this way the insidious system rooted itself in the new State; slave-traders sailed boldly for Africa from the port of Savannah; the trustees, baffled in their humane endeavor, resigned their charter;

and Georgia obeyed the fatal gravitation that has carried her sister States into the slough of slavery.*

General Oglethorpe returned to England in 1743, where he distinguished himself by writing against slavery and the impressment of seamen. In a letter to his friend Granville Sharp he alludes to his former connection with the Colony of Georgia: "My friends and I settled the Colony of Georgia, and by charter were established trustees, to make laws, &c. We determined not to suffer slavery there. But the slave-merchants and their adherents occasioned us not only much trouble, but at last got the then government to favor them. We would not suffer slavery (which is against the Gospel as well as the fundamental law of England) to be authorized under our authority; we refused, as trustees, to make a law permitting such a horrid crime. The government, finding the trustees firmly resolved not to concur with what they believed unjust, took away the charter, by which no law could be passed without our consent." †

We have heard it argued that the system of slavery at the South was *forced* upon a reluctant people in the beginning; but facts, we apprehend, will scarcely warrant the plea. The whole system of colonial slavery was illegal under the law of England; and, though it was fostered in some

* Willson's Am. Hist., pp. 262, 265, 266.

† Stuart's Memoir of Sharp.

instances by government, it appears that nothing stronger than the cupidity of traders, the proclivity to idleness, and the pride of caste among the colonists, gave it footing on our shores. In the North, the more enterprising habits and more solid moral qualities of the people, — uniting with a more stimulating and rigorous climate, — prevented slavery from striking its roots deeply into our social system. But at the South, the predilections of the early immigrants led them to welcome slave labor, and their descendants — influenced by temper and by custom — came to esteem it indispensable to their station, their passions, and their existence.

Thus long before the Revolution two different orders of society were in the process of development in America: one essentially Christian and republican, — recognizing the rights and destiny of human nature; the other essentially Pagan and despotic, — ruthlessly trampling on the prerogatives of man.

III.

STATUS OF SLAVERY IN THE REPUBLIC.

THE discussions that brought on the Revolution, and the struggles and genius by which it was sustained, contributed to raise the republican system into an ascendant position, and to depress its rival in a corresponding. degree.* "It was by no accidental coincidence that the period of the Revolution was the period of a more general and deep-seated opposition to slavery than had been before visible, or than has been witnessed since. The religious sentiment against slavery, as a vio-

* In the original draft of the Declaration of Independence, made by Mr. Jefferson, the following charge is preferred against the king of Great Britain: —

"He has waged cruel war against human nature itself, violating its most sacred rights of life and liberty, in the persons of a distant people who never offended him, captivating and carrying them into slavery in another hemisphere, or to incur miserable death in their transportation thither. This piratical warfare, the opprobrium of infidel powers, is the warfare of the Christian king of Great Britain. Determined to keep a market where men should be bought and sold, he has at length prostituted his negative for suppressing any legislative attempt to prohibit and restrain this execrable commerce."

This paragraph, being objected to by the delegation from Georgia, was expunged from the document. It gives a good indication of the public sentiment of the period touching the turpitude of slave-holding and slave-trading.

2

lation of Heaven-established rights, a sentiment that had been rising for some time previous, and that was now beginning to reach the point of disfellowship with slave-holders, was a sentiment that naturally assimilated itself with the rising opposition to the British government for its invasions of the same sacred rights, and that as naturally sought the same remedy; to wit, the separation of freedom from the embraces of despotic power. . . . . . It is equally evident that the rising opposition of the community in general to the despotic assumptions of the British government, so far as it had anything in it like a manly regard to free principles for its basis, compelled that community to look at the more grievous wrongs of the slaves, and created an earnest sympathy in their favor. A decent regard to self-consistency, in that unsophisticated and earnest age, could scarcely fail to produce some such effects. The only just ground for regret or astonishment is that the spirit of freedom, then seeming to be in the ascendant, did not secure and maintain a more complete and permanent triumph. It is instructive to notice how the spirit of republican liberty and independence, in the different Colonies, was found most predominant and most efficient precisely where there were fewest slaves, and where the spirit of opposition to slavery was likewise most efficient and most predominant; while the regions most deeply involved in the sin of slaveholding, and least accessible to the principles of emancipation, were precisely the same regions in which the apologists and partisans of British usurpation were most numerous and influential, — the regions in which the spirit of opposition to that usurpation was to the smallest extent and with the greatest difficulty roused. The South was overrun with Tories, while New England was united in favor of independence, almost to a man. Particular localities at the North might be mentioned, where the prevalence of slave-holding and slave-trading was connected with a corresponding sympathy with despotic government." *

It is worthy of everlasting remembrance, that almost every patriot who labored conspicuously or efficiently in laying the foundation of the Union was hostile to slavery, realized that it was an incongruous element in the republic, and desired to see it extirpated from the soil of the nation. Still the despotic system was not awed into absolute submission. It was weakened, but not subdued. The finger of destiny seemed clearly to indicate its doom; but it survived, a pensioner on the patience of the hour. It had a few representatives in the Constitutional Convention, who vainly sought to obtain an open recognition of its piratical interests under the federal law.

To the undying glory of the framers of that instrument be it said, no such recognition was obtained. In clear, unequivocal language, the

* Slavery and Anti-Slavery, pp. 69 – 71.

OBJECT of the Constitution is declared to be "to form a more perfect union, establish justice, insure domestic tranquillity, provide for the common defence, promote the general welfare, and secure the blessings of liberty to ourselves and our posterity."

Here is the amplest possible recognition of the interests of REPUBLICAN SOCIETY; but no recognition whatever of the interests of DESPOTIC SOCIETY. If it *was* the real object of the Constitution to "form a more perfect UNION," it could never have contemplated the perpetuity of *two systems* radically antagonistic in their principles and tendencies. If it *was* the real object of the Constitution "to establish JUSTICE," it could not have been intended to protect an institution that perpetrates wholesale and unmitigated *injustice*. And if it *was* the real object of the Constitution "to promote the GENERAL WELFARE, and secure the blessings of LIBERTY," it could never have been designed to indorse any policy that puts the welfare of an entire nation in jeopardy for the sake of fostering the interest of a class, or to sanction a system that reduces one sixth of our population to perpetual servitude.

If we grant that the framers of this great charter knew their own intentions, and honestly meant what their words clearly express, we cannot doubt that the Constitution on which the republic is based was drafted and adopted as the charter of free society, in absolute opposition to every interest of despotism.

The nation having been thus *consecrated* to republican society by the supreme law of the land, all the territory then at the disposal of the Republic was likewise dedicated to freedom.* Express provision had also been made in the Constitution for putting a period to the slave-trade; and the time was fast approaching when that traffic — stigmatized as piracy — would lie under the ban of the nation.

* Hildreth's History, Vol. III. pp. 527, 528.

IV.

THE PROSPECTS OF THE BARONS.

So far all was auspicious. The government of the Union was enthroned in the unqualified interest of freedom; its antecedents, its principles, its instincts, were all hostile to despotic society.* But the government of the Union — competent to reflect the spirit of the Constitution, and to embody the policy of the nation, — had no dominion over the domestic institutions of the States. And in all the States but Massachusetts slavery actually existed at the time the government went into operation, although provision had been made for eventual emancipation in New Hampshire, Connecticut, Rhode Island, and Pennsylvania, and the legal restrictions upon emancipation had been removed in Virginia and in Maryland.†

But the Federal Constitution — moulded in the glow of that ardent devotion to liberty which marked the Revolutionary age, and embodying the

* See a very able argument for the anti-slavery construction of the Constitution, by Rev. Samuel J. May, in the Quarterly Anti-Slavery Magazine, Vol. II. Parts I. and II. of this Essay were written before I met with Mr. May's paper. It gratifies me to find my own views sustained by so admirable an argument as his.

† Hildreth's History, Vol. III. pp. 391, 392.

convictions of men of the widest intelligence and most genuine philanthropy — was really far in *advance* of the mass of the nation. Like Christianity in the Church, it was a Gospel of Liberty in the Republic, far above the practical virtue of the people by whom it had been accepted. While they might honor it with verbal praise, — as men of the world honor the golden rule, as hypocrites honor sanctity, — there was every probability that they would violate its principles in their practical action. And, as Christianity has been degraded to conform to the debasement of human nature, so it might have been expected that this charter of absolute freedom would become *perverted*, under the interpretation of an inferior order of men, to meet the exigencies of a depreciated political morality.

It was only requisite that an insidious hostile interest should be tolerated in some of the States; allowed to work upon public opinion through the cupidity, the pride, the lust and ambition of men; and permitted to creep, through these base avenues, into the halls of national legislation, to effect a virtual revolution in the character and policy of the government, — to metamorphose it into a machinery of despotism; and even to achieve, in process of time, if not checked by a revival of popular virtue, an absolute change in its organic law.

That hostile interest, in the person of slavery, still had its roots or ligaments in all quarters of the Republic; and it only required that the enthusiasm for liberty which the architects of our political temple had felt and inspired should subside in the prosaic routine of prosperous days, to see the instincts of slavery quickened wherever they still survived. Even in the States where it had been abolished by statute, many of the people gave it up with reluctance, and some remained ever after tainted by its evil spirit. These persons from that day to this — *alien* to the genius of the Republic, and wholly subservient to its despotic ANTAGONIST — have been the most efficient servants of the slave power, the most supple apologists for the enormities of slave-holding, the most plausible advocates of the plots of the Southern oligarchy, and the most pernicious enemies of republican society.

Under the influence of the Revolutionary spirit, a strong anti-slavery sentiment was awakened in Delaware, Maryland, and Virginia;* but it yielded to the force of custom, climate, and self-interest, and disappeared, for the most part, with the illustrious men who had fanned it into existence. Washington complains, in a letter addressed to Lafayette, in 1786, that "petitions for the abolition of slavery, presented to the Virginia legislature, could scarcely obtain a hearing." And Jefferson, writing in his old age, laments, with

* It may be stated, on the authority of St. George Tucker, (Professor of Law in William and Mary College, Va.,) that between the years 1782 and 1797 there were upwards of ten thousand private manumissions in Virginia alone.

the pathos of true philanthropic sensibility, the disappointment of his hopes as regards any popular interest in emancipation.

In North Carolina, the subject of abolition was agitated, especially by the Quakers ; but the legislature of that State, backed by a large majority of the people, was unfriendly to their humane views.*

In a word, in nearly all the States where slavery still subsisted, especially in those south of the Potomac, the resolution began to be evinced to *perpetuate* the system at all hazards. From that time the public opinion of foreign nations began to be defied, and that of this country began to be corrupted, in the interest of despotic society.

* Hildreth's History, Vol. III. pp. 393, 394.

V.

PRESTIGE OF THE BARONS. — OMENS. — THE SHIP OF EMPIRE LAUNCHED.

To the eye of the sagacious moralist, it must have been as evident seventy-five years ago as it now is, that slavery cannot be tolerated in a political system like ours, without endangering every institution and prerogative sacred to freemen. Can we conceive of a "powerful oligarchy, possessed of immense wealth," existing in any country without attempting to influence its politics? Since even banking, manufacturing, and commercial capital have been known to interfere with the legitimate course of legislation in many instances, can we apprehend less from slave capital? — especially when it is allowed to accumulate to the enormous sum of two thousand millions of dollars!

Besides, the slave-capitalists are not simply one class in the slave-holding States; they are the DOMINANT CLASS, having positive *control* of the social, religious, and political power of those States. It has been very pertinently observed, that "a weaker prestige, fewer privileges, and less comparative wealth have enabled the British aristocracy to rule England for two centuries, though the root of their strength was cut at Naseby." * Can we fail to see, therefore, that the system of slavery — concentrating, as it does, all political influence in a few men who are virtually absolute in their respective States — becomes a most formidable enemy to free society, and is naturally instigated by the instinct of self-preservation to undermine and overthrow its rival?

Moreover, the temper and manners which slavery continually fosters tend to weaken the securities of freedom. It was well remarked by Dr. Channing,† that "free institutions rest on the love of liberty and the love of order." And "how plain it is that no man can love liberty with a true love who has the heart to wrest it from others! Attachment to freedom does not consist in spurning indignantly a yoke prepared for our own necks; for this is done even by the savage and the beast of prey. It is a moral sentiment, an impartial desire and choice that others as well as ourselves may be protected from every wrong, may be exempted from every unjust restraint. Slave-holding, when perpetuated selfishly and from choice, is at open war with this generous principle. It is a plain, habitual contempt of human rights, and of course impairs that sense of their sanctity which is their best protection. It offers, every day and hour, a precedent of usurpation to the ambitious. It creates a caste with despotic powers; and under

* Philosophy of the Abolition Movement, by Wendell Phillips, p. 38.

† Channing's Works, Vol. II. pp. 85, 86.

such guardians" liberty and justice are about as secure as were the infant princes whom the tyrant smothered in the Tower.

Slavery is equally incompatible with the love of order. It fosters the habit of command, but not the virtue of obedience. The slaveholder is accustomed to see his arbitrary will or changing caprice obeyed by servile multitudes as their supreme law. In the natural growth of his character under this system, he comes to arrogate to himself an authority that transcends the law of the land. The submission he has been accustomed to receive from the slave, he comes to exact of the freeman. His despotic disposition *resisted*, he appeals to *violence*, as he would to execute his plantation-edict. He relies on the bowie-knife and revolver, instead of the magistrate, to enforce his supposed rights. Thus society in all the slave-holding States gravitates toward anarchy. And thus slavery prepares the mind of a community, by its inevitable effects upon sentiments and manners, for the inception of conspiracies that aim at the subversion of the government itself, and the elevation of universal despotism by military violence.*

* "It is evident that there is no way to save our government and render it permanent, but by *constant* resistance to the spirit of despotism, — a spirit whose nature and essence is hostility to free institutions. We should repel its first approaches, reject its alliance, dread its smile, suspect it under the fairest disguises, and always, everywhere, and in every shape, reprobate it as the deadliest foe of republicanism. It is believed that Americans estimate these truths, so far as they relate to foreign despotisms, and are prepared to resist all anti-republican influences from abroad, — excepting always those of

All these dangers, latent in the system of Slavery as a political element, the Federal Government was obliged to *ignore*, when it went into operation. It had to incur the risk. It had to "take the chances." It had to *confide* in the possible virtue

Popery. So jealous are we about *foreign interference* that, let but an Englishman come amongst us, and propose to discuss publicly our own institutions, and at once the outcry is raised, he is an emissary commissioned by despotism to fire the temple of liberty. But the same considerations which call for the exercise of vigilance toward foreign influences, apply with an hundred-fold power to *that despotism* which is in our midst; and yet what is the state of the public mind with regard to the latter? No concern about its existence here, — no suspicion of its character, — not even so much as a misgiving that it has any tendency to sap the foundations of the government, — nay, it is a matter of serious debate whether it be not 'the corner-stone of republicanism'! It is surely time that Americans should investigate the precise bearings of slavery upon our free institutions, — that we should fully understand both the manner in which it endangers them and the imminency of the danger. It will not require great research to see that all the combined power of Europe's aristocracies, monarchies, and despotisms cannot do one tenth part as much to subvert our liberties as our own system of domestic slavery." — *American Slavery* vs. *Liberty, by a Kentuckian*, in *Anti-Slavery Magazine* for Oct. 1836.

This is only an echo of Jefferson's famous words: "The whole commerce between master and slave is a perpetual exercise of the most boisterous passions, the most unremitting despotism, on the one part, and degrading submission on the other. Our children see this, and learn to imitate it; for man is an imitative animal. . . . . . The parent storms, the child looks on, catches the lineaments of wrath, puts on the same airs in the circle of smaller slaves, gives a loose rein to the worst of passions; and, thus nursed, educated, and *daily exercised in* TYRANNY, cannot but be *stamped* by its odious peculiarities. The man must be a prodigy who can retain his manners and morals undepraved by such circumstances. And with what execration should a statesman be loaded, who, permitting one half the citizens to trample on the rights of the other, transforms those into despots and these into enemies, destroys the morals of the one and the *amor patriæ* of the other! And can the liberties of the nation be thought secure, when of the people, in the progress of liberal principles, in the wisdom and integrity of future administrations, and in the merciful overrulings of Divine Providence.

Republican society was not launched under as favorable auspices as many have supposed. Dangerous rocks lay near the channel. Insidious currents waited for the splendid ship. Rapacious pirates lay hidden in quiet lagoons, hoping she might drift within their reach. A shoal of wrangling pilots were struggling for a place at her helm. And so she lifted her anchors, spread forth her canvas, gave her starry flag to the breeze, and sailed away into the untracked Future. And the ghosts of dead Liberties beyond the sea — rising from their sepulchres — wafted after her their solemn "God speed!"

we have removed their only firm basis, — a conviction in the minds of the people that their liberties are the gifts of God, that they are not to be violated but with his wrath? Indeed, I tremble for my country when I reflect that God is just, that his justice cannot sleep forever," &c., &c.

PART II.

OUR POLITICAL APOSTASY.

" Who can reflect, unmoved, upon the round
Of smooth and solemnized complacencies,
By which, on Christian lands, from age to age,
Profession mocks performance. Earth is sick,
And Heaven is weary, of the hollow words
Which states and kingdoms utter when they talk
Of truth and justice."

WORDSWORTH.

"*Casca.* I believe these are portentous things
Unto the climate that they point upon.
"*Cicero.* Indeed, it is a strange-disposed time:
But men may construe things after their fashion,
Clean from the purpose of the things themselves."

SHAKSPEARE, *Julius Cæsar.*

" O masters! if I were disposed to stir
Your hearts and minds to mutiny and rage,
I should do Brutus wrong, and Cassius wrong,
Who, you all know, are honorable men."

Ibid.

" Unhappily, the original policy of the government, and the original principles of the government in respect to slavery, did not permanently control its action. A change occurred,—almost imperceptible at first, but becoming more and more marked and decided, until nearly total." —HON. S. P. CHASE, 1850.

" What, then, have been the causes which have created so new a feeling in favor of slavery in the South,—which have changed the whole nomenclature of the South on the subject,—till it has now become a cherished institution there?"—DANIEL WEBSTER, 1850.

" The general decline of the spirit of liberty that was witnessed in the community, was witnessed also in the Church, and the same moral lethargy and stupor came over them both. The influx of wealth, the erection of castes and aristocracies in society, that displaced simplicity and equality in the State, produced similar effects in the Church. . . . . . The unexpected profitableness of slave labor in the production of cotton was a temptation to the Church, as well as to the rest of the community, and the Southern Church fell into the snare."—WILLIAM GOODELL, 1852.

" The judgment of God will be very visible in infatuating a people ripe and prepared for destruction."—CLARENDON.

I.

THE PROCESS.—THE CAPITAL INFECTED.

WE have seen that the government of the Union was organized in the interest of REPUBLICAN SOCIETY. Under such a government, the interests of despotism could be subserved, and its ultimate ascendency secured, only by an insidious process of corruption and usurpation. That process we are now to describe. It consisted in multiplying slaveholding States, thereby increasing the representative power of slavery in the national legislature; in obtaining a new interpretation of the Constitution; in corrupting the Judiciary; and in depraving the Christian Church.

These changes in the practical working of the government, and in the tone of our ecclesiastical bodies, might be presumed to involve a corresponding degradation of public sentiment, until carried so far as to awaken alarm in the more sagacious of the people, and stimulate resistance and reform.

Moreover, soon after the founding of the government, the interests of freedom came under certain malign influences growing out of the location of the capital in a slave territory. When the District of Columbia was ceded to the United States, all the laws of Maryland heretofore operating on the soil were adopted by Congress in a body, without change or modification. Whoever desires to learn the character of those laws will find them collected in a small work entitled "THE BLACK CODE OF THE DISTRICT OF COLUMBIA."

One law provides a liberal reward for "every person who seizes and takes up a runaway slave." If the individual thus arrested is proved to be a slave, the master pays the reward, together with the "imprisonment fees," when he takes possession of his "property." And if the individual turns out to be a freeman, and no claimant appears, it becomes the duty of the marshal to advertise him, and sell him as a slave, to defray the expenses of his arbitrary arrest and unjust incarceration! Thus the United States, in locating the seat of government on the Potomac, adopted and sanctioned a law under which free and innocent men are deliberately sold into slavery, for the sake of rewarding the kidnapper, and paying the jailer for retaining his victim!

It would be some relief to the national conscience to be permitted to believe that this monstrous law has been a dead letter; but this consolation is not left us. Many freemen have been sold into slavery under its operation. In 1827, 1828, and 1829, the subject was laid before a Congressional committee, from whose report it appears that, during those three years alone, one hundred and seventy-nine persons were committed as fugitives, among whom not less than *twenty-six* were found to be free persons. SIX of these free persons were actually sold into slavery, the rest being saved from that fate only by the humanity of the jailer. Estimating the aggregate fruit of despotism in the District by the development of these three years, aided by the records of the Washington jail, we see how appalling is the turpitude of crime which the nation has committed against the fundamental law of its existence.

There are other laws pertaining to the District, and enjoying the sanction of the Federal authority, which are not less inhuman. Thus, if a slave is caught away from home without a pass, the constable arresting him "*is required to whip him on the bare back at his discretion*, not exceeding *thirty-nine lashes*." For going abroad by night, or riding a horse in the daytime, without permission, he is exposed to "whipping, cropping, or branding in the cheek." For running away, and resisting his pursuers, he may be "shot, killed, and destroyed." Besides these statutes directly affecting the slaves, there are others legalizing a systematic tyranny upon free colored men residing in the District, against distributing publications adverse to slavery, and providing for a special police, at an enormous expense, as "a national guard" in the service of the slave masters.

The establishment of our capital in a slave district thus subjugated to the most barbarous and tyrannical laws to be found on record, has tended to strengthen every aggressive measure by which the despotic system speedily triumphed over the nation. The halls of our legislation and the home of our executive, established in that infected district, became impervious to the nobler influences of the country. The action of Congress became embarrassed — perhaps we may say *controlled* — in important emergencies by local opinion and interest. And, owing to the same influences, Washington City has been, under the thrilling perils of this rebellion, and continues to be at this moment (November, 1861), as rank with the breath of treason as Richmond. If the government is slow to respond to the better impulses of the nation, — if it tenderly admonishes traitors in arms, leaves the Republic to bleed away its life that slavery may continue to exist, and still shields four or five hundred clerks in the Federal offices from the grip of outraged Justice, — we must look for an explanation to the fatal locality of the capital, and to the accursed sorcery that appears to seize most of those who pass its blighting precincts.

II.

TERRITORIAL EXTENSION OF SLAVERY.

THE first slave State admitted into the Union was Kentucky. It was formed of territory originally comprised in the State of Virginia, and naturally adopted her domestic institution.* The admittance of Vermont as a free State, however, preserved the equilibrium of interest in the Republic. Then came Tennessee, originally ceded to the United States by North Carolina, under the proviso "that no regulation made or to be made by Congress shall tend to the emancipation of slaves." The Constitution of Tennessee adopted the code of North Carolina, thus "tacitly legalizing the system of slavery," while avoiding a direct allusion to the subject.†

The acquisition of Louisiana and Florida — though of obvious value, in a commercial point of view, to the whole country — opened immense fields for the propagation of slavery, and greatly

* It seems, however, that, "in the Convention that formed the Constitution of Kentucky, in 1780, the effort to prohibit slavery was nearly successful." "But for the interest of two large slaveholders — Messrs. Breckinridge and Nicholson — the measure, it is believed, would have been carried." — *Power of Congress*, p. 34.

† Hildreth's History, Vol. IV. pp. 150, 632.

enhanced the influence of the *despotic interest* in the nation.

But the application of Missouri marks the rise of the great controversy among us on the extension of slavery. Already four slave States — Kentucky, Tennessee, Louisiana, and Mississippi — had been admitted, with little debate or opposition, — being offset against an equal number of free States, namely, Vermont, Ohio, Indiana, and Illinois. But, as Alabama was about to come in as a slave State, it was very reasonably demanded — in accordance with the rule hitherto observed — that slavery should be prohibited in Missouri. Accordingly, Mr. TALLMADGE moved, in the House, to insert a clause in the bill relative to Missouri, "prohibiting any further introduction of slaves, and granting freedom to the children of those already there on their attaining the age of twenty-five." This motion, after an exciting debate of three days, was carried by a small majority. The bill went to the Senate, where it received such amendments as the House refused to adopt, and so was lost. A similar effort, made at the same time, to organize the Territory of Arkansas under a clause prohibiting slavery, failed to secure even the vote of the House. At no distant day, both States came into the Union, without any restriction upon the system of slavery; and the *balance* of territorial weight, thus inclined in favor of despotism, has never been restored.

It was during this first debate on the Missouri

question, or rather after the defeat of the prohibitory clause in the Arkansas Bill, that the celebrated *compromise line*, dividing the territory west of the Mississippi, was first proposed. As originally suggested, that line was to follow the northern boundary of Arkansas; * but its final adoption was made dependent on the admission of Missouri as a slave State. Nor did it prove, even then, a barrier to the aggressive cupidity of the slave-holders, as the duplicity of two administrations and the wrongs of Kansas impressively testify.

While the slave-holding propaganda were struggling to bind Missouri to their empire, they began to covet a new province belonging to a sister republic.† The annexation of Texas began to be openly agitated in the South and West as far back as 1829, and the motives that inspired the movement were boldly avowed. It was argued, about this time, in a series of papers attributed to a gentleman who subsequently occupied a seat in the Senate of the United States, that the acquisition of that extensive domain would add five or six slave-holding States to the Union, or even nine States as large as Kentucky. "In Virginia, about the same time, calculations were made as to the increased value which would thus be given to slaves, and it was even said that this acquisition would raise the price fifty per cent." ‡ Thus

* Hildreth, Vol. VI. pp. 661, 662. † Ibid. p. 713.

‡ Dr. Channing's Letter on the Annexation of Texas, Works, Vol. II. p. 218.

would be opened a new market for the sale of human beings; and thus another "vast accession of political power" would be secured to the slave-holding despotism. "The project of dismembering a neighboring republic, that slave-holders and slaves might overspread a region which had been consecrated to a free population, was discussed in newspapers as coolly as if it were a matter of obvious right and unquestionable humanity." *

The sinuous intrigues and impudent frauds by which Mexico was robbed of this province,† with a view to its ultimate annexation to the Union, as another contribution to the already preponderating influence of slavery, have become matters of historical certainty; and the fact that this measure created so little alarm in the free States, at the time it was being consummated, affords one proof out of many, that we had become infatuated with the lust of empire, and that the sentiment of liberty had become torpid in the nation.

In vain a few men at the North, not wholly blind to the purposes and tendencies of slavery, raised an indignant voice in protest, — as had been done, indeed, during the sacrifice of Missouri; but the baleful project had acquired too great an *impetus* to be arrested. Mr. Wendell Phillips relates — and we quote the incident to illustrate the fatal blindness of the North — "being one of a committee which waited on Abbott Lawrence,

* Dr. Channing's Letter, Works, Vol. II. p. 198.

† North American Review for July, 1836.

a year or two only before annexation, to ask his countenance to some general movement, without distinction of party, against the Texas scheme. He smiled at our fears," says MR. PHILLIPS, "begged us to have no apprehensions; stating that his correspondence with leading men at Washington enabled him to assure us annexation was impossible, and that the South itself was determined to defeat the project. A short time after, Senators and Representatives from Texas took their seats in Congress." *

Thus the relative positions of the two systems of society were changed.

At the formation of the Union, REPUBLICAN SOCIETY was in the ascendant, — all its interests guaranteed by the supreme law of the nation. Now, DESPOTIC SOCIETY was in the ascendant, having the government under its control, and prostituting all the energies of the Republic to the extension of the blighting curse of human bondage.

Once, the States contiguous to those which had abolished slavery — smitten by the sterility and ignorance which the system entails, and viewing across the border the salutary results of freedom — were turning their thoughts towards emancipation. Their proximity to States flourishing under free labor, and ennobled by every element of social progress, was gradually forcing upon their

* Philosophy of the Abolition Movement, p. 24.

reluctant minds the propriety of adopting the more humane and prosperous system. But the opening of immense territories in the Southwest to the cupidity of slavery at once arrested the tendency to emancipation in the border States.*

The almost unlimited demand for slave labor on the rice, sugar, and cotton plantations of those new territories, gave a fearful impulse to the rearing of slaves in the old States, and opened a domestic trade in the bodies and souls of our fellow-creatures, as infamous, to say the least, as it was lucrative.

Thus slavery — once apparently in the last stage of dissolution in Virginia and Kentucky, in Delaware and Maryland — *revived* in a more virulent character, and assumed a more shameful attitude than ever, in those States, while it spread its mortal blight, by successive aggressions, and by the wicked complicity of a majority of the American people, over the fairest regions of the continent.

* See this view sustained by Justice McLean in his argument in the Dred Scott case.

III.

SLAVE REPRESENTATION.

LET us now observe more particularly how the increase of slaves, and consequently of slave representation, was made to affect the political action of the country.

When the principle of slave representation was proposed to be admitted into the Constitution, it was indignantly resisted; nor was the principle finally conceded to the South until coupled with another, providing that their proportion of the direct taxes that might be levied should be increased in the ratio of such representation. This proviso was probably designed to operate as a practical check upon the inordinate growth of slave representation; and at the same time to relieve the Constitution of the odium of recognizing any interest peculiar to slavery.* Such, however, has

* The views of Rev. S. J. May upon this clause in the Constitution — which I had not read when this part of my essay was penned — appear to me quite original and worthy of note. While the remarks of my esteemed friend do not affect anything which I have said in this section concerning the pernicious consequences of slave representation, they *do* vindicate the framers of the Constitution from any *design* to favor the system of slavery, when they admitted the clause in question. See *Quarterly Anti-Slavery Magazine*, pp. 80 – 82.

not been the effect, and the case presents an instructive example of the fact, that no compromise with injustice, for the sake of avoiding a present difficulty, and in the specious assurance of a remote advantage, ever fulfils its flattering promise.

In the several States, before their union under the Federal compact, it had been customary to provide for debts and expenditures by *direct taxation;* and it was naturally enough supposed that, under the new government, a large part of the revenue would be furnished by the same process. But, in point of fact, — "with the exception of two brief periods, during the French war, and the war with England, — the revenue of the United States has been raised by *duties on imports.* The greatest proportion of these duties are, of course, paid by the free States; for here, the poorest laborer daily consumes several articles of foreign production, of which from one eighth to one half the price is a tax paid to government. The clothing of the slave population increases the revenue very little, and their food almost none at all."

Thus, in the practical operation of our government, the South has obtained all the advantages of the proviso for slave representation, while furnishing scarcely any of the anticipated equivalent. The effect of the arrangement upon the fortunes of the slaves has been peculiarly aggravating, for — since the prerogative of slave representation has always been used to extend the slave power — the slaves have been practically made to vote for the perpetuity of slavery, and to "furnish halters to hang their own posterity." *

The immeasurable advantage which this prerogative has given to the South, in a political point of view, was forcibly expressed, many years ago, by a Southern gentleman, the HON. W. B. SEABROOK. In a pamphlet on the management of slaves, he is said to have used this language: "An addition of one million of dollars to the private fortune of DANIEL WEBSTER, would not give to Massachusetts more influence than she now possesses in the Federal councils. On the other hand, *every increase of slave property in South Carolina* is a fraction thrown into the scale *by which her representation in Congress is determined.*"

As far back as 1833, the importance of the slave element, as an instrument of political ascendency, was well understood at the South, and by a few men at the North. In a speech made in Congress that year, by MR. CLAYTON of Georgia, he boldly alluded to the slave population as "the machinery of the South." Upwards of twenty members had already obtained seats in the House of Representatives by virtue of slave representation. In a speech made three days later, JOHN QUINCY ADAMS declared, that, tracing the history of the government from its foundation, "it would be easy to prove that its *decisions* had been affected in general by less majorities

* Mrs. Child.

than that." He would go even further, he said, and insist that the slave representation had ever been, in fact, THE RULING POWER OF THE GOVERNMENT.

"The history of the Union has afforded a continual proof," said MR. ADAMS, "that this representation of property, which they enjoy as well in the election of President and Vice-President of the United States as upon the floor of the House of Representatives, has secured to the slave-holding States *the entire control of* THE NATIONAL POLICY, and, almost without exception, the possession of the highest executive office of the Union. Always united in the purpose of regulating the affairs of the whole Union by the standard of the slave-holding interest, their disproportionate numbers in the electoral colleges have enabled them, in ten out of twelve quadrennial elections, to confer the chief magistracy upon one of their own citizens. Their suffrages at every election, without exception, have been almost exclusively confined to a candidate of their own caste. Availing themselves of the divisions which, from the nature of man, always prevail in communities entirely free, they have sought and found *auxiliaries* in the other quarters of the Union, by associating the passions of parties and the ambition of individuals with their own purposes, to establish and maintain throughout the confederated nation the slave-holding policy." *

* Speech on the Tariff, Feb. 4, 1833.

In palpable confirmation of these statements, the offices of President of the United States, President of the Senate, Speaker of the House of Representatives, and Chief Justice of the United States, were all occupied by incumbents from the South, — pledged to the slave-holding policy, — at the very time MR. ADAMS was speaking.

The most lamentable effect of this political advantage, this *imperium in imperio*, has been experienced in the corruption of Northern politicians. Since the South was always certain to be united on every important question, while the North has ever been more or less divided; and since the prerogative of slave representation has given to the South, from the beginning, the controlling power in the government, — it has generally been found necessary for politicians from the free States to affiliate with the purposes of the South, and to adopt its policy, in order to obtain any offices of honor or emolument in the Federal Union.

Thus the path of ambition for Northern members of Congress has been, almost of necessity, the path of subserviency and compromise. The highest Federal honors were accessible only to those who paid fealty to the slave-holders, and abased themselves most as the tools of their arbitrary policy. In a Republic nominally the freest on the globe, the positions of supreme dignity and trust, the executive and administrative offices, could be won only by bowing to the dictation of an oligarchy, and becoming ductile to the crafty designs of a despotism. Shameful and ominous are the anomalies which our political history has developed. A vile interest, originally lurking in the recesses of the State, and abandoned to die of its own virulence, — an interest under the ban of public opinion the civilized world over, and no man so lost to virtue as to plead for it, — an *excrescence*, the outgrowth of Asiatic depravity and of feudal manners, alien alike to the new nation and the new age, — an abominable thing, condemned by equity, and abhorred by nature, — is warmed into vital action by a fatal conjunction of circumstances, encouraged to emerge into the public arena, and promoted, in process of time, to hold the balance of power in the greatest of republican governments! The leading statesmen of the country — lured by the sin the angels are said to have fallen by — are seen quenching the light of conscience, killing the instincts native to freemen, and stooping to render homage to the mother of villanies. And the fame of many an illustrious son of freedom, nurtured by generous scholarship, crowned by classic eloquence, and applauded by confiding States, is seen blighted by the curse that lights on the betrayer of humanity, and turned into fuel to blazon the base man's shame!

IV.

SLAVERY CONSTRUING THE CONSTITUTION.

WHILE the immense territorial acquisitions were contributing to the ascendency of the DESPOTIC SYSTEM, the same dangerous tendency was being accelerated by a new doctrine of constitutional interpretation. This doctrine, by successive stages of growth, extending through seventy years of political intrigue and corruption, has become the most gigantic and impudent sophistry that was ever imposed upon a rational public.

It has virtually transformed the Constitution into a *national slave-code*, — perverting it into a broad warrant for slave-holding and kidnapping in every State and Territory of the Union, — degrading the judges of the Supreme Court to the level of a political club, and changing the President of the United States into a pettifogger, pleading in the interest of the Southern oligarchy. The authority of most of the courts, and the inordinate influence of a single Northern statesman, have prevailed so far as to secure a general acceptance of the new dogma in the Free States. And yet the judicial authorities are notoriously at variance on the question of constitutional interpretation, — a

3*

minority of the judges of the Supreme Court of the United States arguing for the anti-slavery construction, in opposition to their colleagues;* and even MR. WEBSTER, whose authority as expounder of our national law it has long been the fashion to venerate, was not always consistent with his own decisions.

The question is not of so profound or complex a nature as to prevent men of ordinary intelligence, and of little legal learning, from deducing a sound conclusion. It is only needful to recall a few cardinal facts to convince any person, willing to be guided by common sense, that the Constitution is not responsible for the system of slavery.

In the celebrated decision of the Court of King's Bench, pronounced by LORD MANSFIELD in the case of James Somersett, in 1772, — a decision which has never been reversed, — it was shown that slavery was nowhere legalized by the law of England. "The state of slavery is of such a nature," said LORD MANSFIELD, "that it is incapable of being introduced on any reasons, moral or political, but only by positive law. It is so *odious* that nothing can be suffered to support it but positive law."

According to this decision, slavery never had a *legal* existence in the American Colonies, so long as they were subject to the law of England. It was *tolerated*, but was never lawful. When these Colonies came to be united in the Federal compact,

* See the Arguments of Justices McLean and Curtis, in the case of Dred Scott.

after the Revolution, it became necessary, in order to give slavery a legal existence in the Republic, to enact into the Constitution a positive provision for its support. Being of such an exceptional nature, nothing short of an express and positive enactment could bring it under the protection of the General Government. Can any such enactment be found? So far from it, neither the word *slave* nor *slavery* occurs in the instrument. The history of the formation of the Constitution shows that these terms were excluded, not by accident, but by design, — so strenuously opposed were the majority of its framers to any recognition of the system. Indeed, as DR. CHANNING has said, "a stranger might read it without suspecting the existence of this institution among us." And so free is the Constitution from any direct reference to the system, that, if slavery were abolished throughout the States, not a single article or section of the instrument would require revision.

In the absence, then, of every provision for the support of slavery in the supreme law of the land, how is it possible to claim for it a guaranty in the Constitution, as a national interest, — it being, in its nature, "so odious that nothing can be suffered to support it but positive law"?

In view of the considerations just submitted, let us now consider the famous clause concerning the rendition of fugitives, — that Malakoff of the slaveholders, in the shelter of which the Fugitive-Slave

Bill was framed. The history of that clause is thus related by MR. HILDRETH: "When the article came up providing for the mutual delivery of fugitives from justice, a motion was made by BUTLER, seconded by C. PINCKNEY, that fugitive slaves and servants be included. WILSON objected that this would require a delivery at the public expense. SHERMAN saw no more propriety in the public seizing and surrendering a servant than a horse. BUTLER withdrew his motion; but the next day introduced a substitute, evidently borrowed from an ordinance of Congress passed a few days before, and — in its strong resemblance to one of the clauses of the old New England Articles of Union — bearing plain marks of a New England hand. *Agreed to without debate*, it became, with some subsequent changes of phraseology, that famous clause which provides that 'no person held to service or labor in one State, under the laws thereof, escaping into another, shall, in consequence of any law or regulation therein, be discharged from such service or labor, but shall be delivered up on claim of the party to whom such service or labor may be due.'" *

Now that allusion is made, in this clause, to fugitive slaves, as well as to indented servants, is barely possible; and yet it seems that the original motion, in which the word *slaves* occurs, was not suffered to pass. No open and unequivocal concession of this claim to hunt fugitive slaves was

* History of the United States, Vol. III. p. 522.

admitted into the Constitution. And the fact that BUTLER'S substitute (in which the word *slaves* had been struck out) was accepted *without debate*, seems to indicate that the anti-slavery members of the Convention attached some different meaning to the clause, or believed that its ambiguity would disarm it of practical force.

Admitting that this clause refers to fugitive slaves, it may well be doubted whether it was designed to express more than a recommendation to the States, in the nature of comity. It is pertinent to this case to remember, that the civil law, throughout the continent of Europe, without a single known exception, has decided "that slavery can exist only within the territory where it has been expressly established; and that if a slave escapes or is carried beyond such territory, his master cannot reclaim him unless by virtue of some express stipulation.* There is no nation in Europe which considers itself bound to return to his master a fugitive slave, under the civil law or the law of nations. On the contrary, the slave is held to be free where there is no treaty obligation, or compact in some other form, to return him to his master." † Whether the obscure clause in question amounts to such a "stipulation," or

* See Grotius, lib. 2, chap. 15, 5, 1; lib. 10, chap. 10, 2, 1; Wicquopost's Ambassador, lib. 1, p. 418: 4 Martin, 385; Case of the Creole in the House of Lords, 1842; 1 Phillimore on International Law, 316, 335, — cited by Justice McLean.

† Argument of Justice McLean in Reports of the Supreme Court, Vol. XIX. p. 534.

"treaty," which the Constitution arms the General Government with power to execute, may fairly admit of doubt.*

Again: the supposed right to reclaim fugitive slaves is grounded on the Federal compact, to which the North and South became voluntary partners. Now what is the orthodox doctrine in relation to the *conditions* that render this compact *binding?* We will be guided here by MR. WEBSTER, the great "expounder" of our constitutional law and of the duty of the States. In a speech made at Capon Springs, in 1851, MR. WEBSTER said: "It would be absurd to suppose that either the North or the South has the power or the right to violate any part of the Constitution, and then claim from the other observance of its provisions.

* The "doubt" expressed above has been confirmed by the following:—

"We frankly confess, that it is less easy to give to this article than to any other in the Constitution such an exposition as will reconcile it with the avowed sentiments and purposes of the framers. This difficulty has been enhanced, if not created, however, by the subsequent action of Congress under this article. We refer to the Act of 1793, for the recapture of fugitive slaves. There was then, no doubt, an arrangement made by the General Government to assist those who have the hardihood to hold their fellow-beings as property to retake them as such, if they flee for refuge from oppression into a free State. But for this the Congress of 1793 alone are responsible, not the Convention of 1788. The Act has recently been pronounced. by a distinguished Judge of one of the State Courts, unconstitutional; and we have no doubt that it is so. Congress could have no authority in the premises, other than that conveyed in the article before us. Now, we look into this in vain to find any right which our national legislature had to enact a law regulating the recapture of a fugitive slave from any State, more than it would have had to enact a law providing in what

If the South were to violate any part of the Constitution, would the North be any longer bound by it? and if the North were deliberately to violate any part of it, would the South be bound any longer to observe its obligation? How absurd it would be to suppose, when different parties enter into a compact for certain purposes, that either can disregard any one provision, and expect the other to observe it!"

Here the doctrine of constitutional obligation is very clearly set forth, by a jurist eminently qualified, in the estimation of the public, to illumine the dark subject. It matters not that this principle was laid down in the course of an argument for the Fugitive-Slave Bill; if it is sound, we are as much entitled to the use of it as MR. WEBSTER.

way persons shall be held to service in any State. The Congress of 1793, with equal propriety, might have passed an act for the abolition of slavery. The members of that body transcended their powers. All that the framers of the Constitution had done, or could be persuaded to do, was so to construct the article now under our consideration, that those who are held to service in any State may be retaken there, if they can be. But if it leaves to the several States to prescribe how persons may or shall be held to service or labor there, it equally leaves to the several States to prescribe how the claims to the fugitive shall be preferred and proved. In short, the Constitution does leave the responsibility of holding slaves where it was found, and expresses no intention to make the national government any way subservient to its support." — REV. S. J. MAY.

This question would seem to be placed beyond controversy by the testimony of Mr. Madison: —

"On motion of Mr. Randolph, the word *servitude* was struck out, and *service* unanimously inserted, — the *former* being thought to express the condition of *slaves*, and the *latter* the obligation of *free persons*." — *Madison Papers*, Vol. III. p. 1569.

See, also, Goodell, "Slavery and Anti-Slavery," pp. 227 - 231.

The doctrine is, that if either the North or the South deliberately violate any part of the Constitution, the compact ceases to be binding upon the other party. Now let us see which party it was that first violated the Constitution. As far back as 1825, before any complaint had been uttered against the Northern agitators, — before the Abolitionists had fulminated their thunders, or "the under-ground railroad" had been laid, — "the Legislature of South Carolina passed an act legalizing the imprisonment of colored persons who should enter her boundaries, and their sale, in case of inability to pay their jail-fees." Now, at the adoption of the Federal Constitution, colored persons were in the enjoyment of the right of the elective franchise in not less than five of the States, and were of course included among the "people" who voted to adopt that instrument.* That act of the South Carolina Legislature was, therefore, a palpable violation of the provision in the Federal Constitution which declares that "the citizens of each State shall be entitled to *all* the privileges and immunities of citizens in the several States." It is a well-known fact, that, in both South Carolina and Louisiana, colored seamen from the North were exposed to imprisonment and to sale from the auction block in payment of their jail-fees, if found in the ports of Charleston and New Orleans. With a view to

* Argument of Curtis, Reports of the Supreme Court, Vol. XIX. p. 574.

obtaining legal redress against this perfidious treatment of her colored citizens, by taking an appeal to the Supreme Court of the United States, the Legislature of Massachusetts, after repeated efforts to induce Southern lawyers to make the necessary legal investigations, sent two of her own citizens as agents to those cities. Both gentlemen were expelled, at no little personal peril, and the Legislature of South Carolina, glorying in the act of high-handed despotism which the Charleston mob had achieved, proceeded to pass a statute making it a penal offence, punishable in the State prison, for an agent of Massachusetts to enter that State in pursuit of legal redress in behalf of her colored citizens.

Thus it should seem, agreeably to the principle laid down by DANIEL WEBSTER himself, that, if the fugitive clause in the Constitution be never so binding upon the North, by virtue of the Federal compact, *the North had become absolved of all obligation to respect it* long before the Fugitive-Slave Bill was enacted, *in consequence of repeated violations of the compact by the South.* "How absurd it would be to suppose," quoth MR. WEBSTER, "when different parties enter into a compact for certain purposes, that either can disregard any one provision, and expect the other to observe it!"

But grant the late interpretation of this clause to be correct, and grant that the constitutional obligation was still binding when the Fugitive-

Slave Bill was being framed, — in what part of the Constitution do we find authority for hunting fugitive slaves at the public cost; for "magnifying slave property above all other property" in the Union; for denying the trial by jury; for suspending the writ of *habeas corpus;* and for offering a bribe to the Commissioner to incline his decision in favor of the kidnapper?

However men may differ as to the meaning or scope of the fugitive clause, or its permanent validity, there can hardly be two opinions in reference to the palpable unconstitutionality of this bill of abominations, professedly framed under its sanction. The Constitution provides that in suits at common law, when the value in controversy shall exceed twenty dollars, the right of trial by jury shall be preserved, yet the bill in question, in a suit that involves the total value of a human being, abrogates this right. The Constitution provides that the privilege of the writ of *habeas corpus* shall not be suspended, unless when in cases of rebellion or invasion the public safety may require it, yet the execution of this odious bill does suspend this time-honored prerogative of free States. The Constitution was adopted to establish justice, and secure the blessings of liberty, and yet the Fugitive-Slave Bill offers five dollars to the Commissioner if he decide in favor of personal liberty, and ten dollars if he decide in favor of the slave-hunter. How can we doubt that this was a statute made, not in the spirit of mutual compromise and comity between the States, but in the interest of an aggressive oligarchy? It was an impudent and flagrant *usurpation* of powers not granted by the Constitution, for the purpose of promoting the ascendency of DESPOTIC SOCIETY.

V.

SLAVERY IN THE SUPREME COURT.

NOT less violent and arbitrary was the construction forced upon the Constitution in the dogmas announced by the Supreme Court under the memorable decision in the case of DRED SCOTT *v.* SANDFORD. Those dogmas deny the power of Congress to establish territorial governments,— pronounce null and void the prohibition of slavery north of thirty-six degrees thirty minutes, embodied in the Missouri Compromise,— and affirm that the *status* of slavery attaches to the slave, wherever he may be carried by his master.

That these positions are utterly untenable has been ably shown in the arguments of the two dissenting Judges; and it seems impossible for a disinterested person to examine the tissue of sophisms with which Chief Justice TANEY and the associate Judges concurring with him build up their case, without perceiving that those opinions are only the pleas of so many pettifoggers, pledged, not to the service of the Republic, but to the interest of the slave-holders.

These dogmas announced by the Supreme Court are of a nature which any man is competent to test, who may take the trouble to institute the necessary research. In relation to the jurisdiction of Congress over the Territories, Justice McLean, dissenting from the Court, says: "The judicial mind of this country, State and Federal, has agreed on no subject, within its legitimate action, with equal unanimity, as on the power of Congress to establish Territorial governments. No court, State or Federal, no judge or statesman, is known to have had any doubts on this question for nearly sixty years after the power was exercised. Such governments have been established from the sources of the Ohio to the Gulf of Mexico, extending to the lakes on the north and the Pacific Ocean on the west, and from the lines of Georgia to Texas. Great interests have grown up under the territorial laws over a country more than five times greater in extent than the original thirteen States; and these interests — corporate or otherwise — have been cherished and consolidated by a benign policy, without any one supposing the law-making power had united with the judiciary — under the universal sanction of the whole country — to usurp a jurisdiction which did not belong to them. Such a discovery at this late date is more extraordinary than anything which has occurred in the judicial history of this or any other country." *

So, in relation to the alleged illegality of the Missouri Compromise, the Chief Justice and his

* Reports of the Supreme Court, Vol. XIX. p. 545.

indorsers seem to be equally wide of the mark. The prohibition of slavery north of thirty-six degrees thirty minutes and of the State of Missouri, contained in the act admitting that State into the Union, was passed in the House of Representatives, by a vote of 134 to 42. Before giving his signature to the act, Mr. MUNROE submitted it to his Cabinet, and they held the restriction of slavery in a Territory to be within the constitutional powers of Congress.* Indeed, such power had been assumed without question, as early as 1804, when Congress prohibited the introduction of slaves into Orleans Territory from any other part of the Union, under the penalty of freedom to the slave.†

But in no dogma announced by the Chief Justice does he make so flagrant an assault upon the principles and spirit of the Constitution, as in that in which he maintains that *the* STATUS *of slavery adheres to the slave*, wherever the master may convey him, — in other words, that the Constitution guarantees protection to property in slaves, as to all other property, *wherever its authority is acknowledged.*

The extraordinary nature of this assumption will be appreciated at a glance, when we consider the undisputed fact, that the state of slavery has been viewed — for almost a century past, by the courts of England, America, and all other civilized nations — as a mere municipal regulation,

* Reports of the Supreme Court, Vol. XIX. p. 546.
† Ibid., p. 544.

founded upon, and limited to the range of, the local laws by which it was established.*

Now if slavery be limited to the range of the local laws especially ordained for its support, — which is the unanimous doctrine of the jurists in all countries, — "how can the slave" — in the language of Justice McLean — "be coerced to serve in a State or Territory, not only without the authority of law, but against its express provisions? What gives the master the right to control the will of his slave? The local law, which exists in some form. But where there is no such law, can the master control the will of the slave by force? Where no slavery exists, the presumption, without regard to color, is in favor of freedom. Under such a jurisdiction, may the colored man be levied on as the property of his master by a creditor? On the decease of the master, does the slave descend to his heirs as property? Can the master sell him? Any one or all of these acts may be done to the slave where he is legally held to service. But where the law does not confer this power, it cannot be exercised. Lord Mansfield held that a slave brought into England was free. Lord Stowell agreed with Lord Mansfield in this respect, and that the slave could not be coerced in England. . . . . . By virtue of what law is it, that a master may take his slave into free territory, and exact from him the duties of a slave? The law of the territory does not sanction it. No

* Reports of the Supreme Court, Vol. XIX. p. 547.

authority can be claimed under the Constitution of the United States, or any law of Congress. Will it be said that the slave is taken as property, — the same as other property which the master may own? To this I answer, that colored persons are made property by the law of the State, and no such power has been given to Congress." *

It is worthy of note, that every other description of property which a man might bring to England from one of her slave islands was protected by law. The property in the slave was not protected, because there was no law in England that recognized slavery. How clearly this shows "that property in a human being does not arise from nature, or from the common law," but, in the language of the courts, is a "mere municipal regulation," having no other authority than the local laws especially instituted to protect it!

In this amazing effort of the Chief Justice of the United States to pervert the Federal Constitution into a virtual slave-code, extending its infamous sanctions over the entire republic, — the wicked audacity of the slave propaganda was thought to have culminated. In that decision, the long series of usurpations against liberty — the long succession of arrogant and tyrannical concessions, extorted from free society — seemed to receive an ominous consummation.

* Reports of the Supreme Court, Vol. XIX. p. 548.

VI.

SLAVERY SUBDUING THE CHURCH.

THE account we have undertaken to give of our national apostasy would be incomplete, without a notice of the change that took place in the sentiment of the Church, as regards the sinfulness of slave-holding, and its growing toleration and approval of the practice.

The views that characterized a great majority of our statesmen in the Revolutionary period may fairly be said to have honored also the leading clergy. It has been even supposed that the decided anti-slavery sentiments of WASHINGTON, JEFFERSON, FRANKLIN, and others, may be traced to the influence of DR. HOPKINS whose celebrated "Dialogue" was published in 1776, and to that of DR. JONATHAN EDWARDS of New Haven (afterwards President of Union College, Schenectady), who preached a powerful sermon before the Connecticut Society for the Promotion of Freedom, in 1791. The work of DR. HOPKINS was circulated extensively during the Revolutionary period, "and is known to have produced a powerful impression upon the minds of reflecting men, including some in high stations." The boldness and pungency of

Dr. Edwards's sermon may be conceived by the fact, that he "distinctly charges upon the slaveholder the crime of man-stealing, and the repetition of the crime every day he continues to hold a slave in bondage. He charges him also with 'theft or robbery,' — nay, with 'a greater crime than fornication, theft, or robbery.' He predicts that, if we may judge the future by the past, within fifty years from this time it will be as shameful for a man to hold a negro slave, as to be guilty of common robbery or theft! In an appendix, Dr. Edwards answers objections against immediate emancipation, just as modern Abolitionists answer them now."*

The character of these publications, and the favorable reception they met with from the public, indicate beyond controversy the *position of the* Church, at that time, toward American slavery. The doctrine of Abolition was unquestionably in the ascendant.

The sentiments of the Methodist societies, at that time, were expressed both in the well-known opinions of Wesley and in the minutes of the Conference for the year 1780. "The Conference acknowledges that slavery is contrary to the laws of God, man, and nature, — hurtful to society, — contrary to the dictates of conscience and pure religion, ... and they pass their disapprobation upon all our friends who keep slaves, and they

* Goodell's "Slavery and Anti-Slavery," pp. 92, 93.

advise their freedom." * In 1785, the Methodist Episcopal Church held this language: "We hold in the deepest abhorrence the practice of slavery, and shall not cease to seek its destruction, by all wise and prudent means." Similar sentiments were held by the General Assembly of the Presbyterian Church, and by the Baptist denomination.

The story of the subsequent decline of this righteous sentiment in the Church — the story of its toleration of slave-holding, of its acquiescence in all the practices which it involves, of its final approbation of the system, and its open assaults upon the few surviving sons of Liberty — will comprise, in coming time, the most dishonorable chapter of our annals, and will rank among the most dubious records of Christian history. We shall cite such facts in this section of the essay — from the proceedings of different ecclesiastical bodies — as we deem needful to convey an accurate impression of this melancholy declension, — not exhausting the materials we have collected, but culling from them as copiously as our limits admit.

We will first notice the declension of Christian sentiment in the METHODIST EPISCOPAL CHURCH. In 1801, the General Conference declared, "We are *more than ever convinced* of the great evil of African slavery, which still exists in these United

* Sunderland's Anti-Slavery Manual, p. 58.

States." In 1836, the same Conference declared that they "*wholly disclaim any right*, WISH, *or intention*, to interfere with the civil and political relation of master and slave, as it exists in the slave-holding States of this Union."

This is about as complete a somerset of opinion as we could expect an ecclesiastical body to execute in thirty-five years; but here is another equally dexterous.

In 1797, the General Conference had *required* its preachers to memorialize their legislatures in favor of Abolition. But in the Pastoral Address issued in 1836, the same Conference, *dissuading* their members from agitating the subject, inform them that "The question of slavery in the United States, by the constitutional compact which binds us together as a nation, is left to be regulated by the several State legislatures themselves; and thereby is put beyond the control of the general government, *as well as of all ecclesiastical bodies*," &c. The Conference omits to mention *what* "constitutional compact" had been formed since 1797, when the ministry were expressly required to use their influence against slavery. It also neglects to explain *why* — if the responsibility of maintaining slavery rests with the State legislatures — it has *ceased to be proper* to memorialize them on the subject. In 1785, this Church "held in the deepest abhorrence the practice of slavery," and were resolved "not to cease to seek its destruction"; but in 1836 they disclaim the right, the wish, and the intention to interfere with it.

In 1839, Bishop SOULE, at the Pittsburg Conference, declared, "I have never yet advised the liberation of a slave, and think I never shall." In 1838, "Bishop HEDDING, presiding at the New England Conference, refused to put resolutions condemning the buying and selling of slaves, and at the same time refused to put a motion declaring slavery to be a moral evil." *

The Book Concern owned by this denomination, "up to the division which followed the General Conference of 1844, published books for the whole connection, North and South; hence, in the republication of English works which have contained allusions to slavery, various expedients were resorted to to render them acceptable to slaveholders. Sometimes the anti-slavery matter is said to have been expunged; and in other cases it has been attempted to explain it away by notes appended by the American Book-room editor." †

Soon after the secession of the Wesleyan members of this Church, on account of its approbation of slavery, a division took place between its Northern and Southern sections. "The action of the General Conference which led to the separation was not against slavery or slave-holding by the membership or ministers, but simply against slaveholding by the Episcopacy; and that not upon

* Goodell's "Slavery and Anti-Slavery," pp. 144 – 148.

† True Wesleyan, January 24, 1852.

principle, but wholly upon the ground of expediency." The rupture, moreover, "did not throw all the slave States into the Southern General Conference. Official documents show that there are at the present time in the Northern General Conference eight annual conferences a part or the whole of whose territory is in the slave-holding States. There are many slave-holding preachers in the Methodist Episcopal Church, and it ordains slave-holders to the ministry. It is computed that there are in the Methodist Episcopal Church North not less than four thousand slave-holders, and twenty-seven thousand slaves."

The quotation is from the Annual Report of the American and Foreign Anti-Slavery Society for 1850. It is proper to add, that in 1849 and 1850 there seems to have been a revival of anti-slavery sentiment, or at least of anti-slavery *action*, in the Northern branch of this Church, — judging by certain resolutions then adopted, which denounce slavery in severe terms, and conclude by affirming "that the glory of God and the good of mankind require the exclusion of slave-holders from the Christian Church."

We next notice the declension of Christian sentiment in the PRESBYTERIAN CHURCH. In 1794 this Church had denounced slave-holding as "man-stealing." "In 1815 the General Assembly declared their 'approbation of the principles of civil liberty,' and their 'deep concern at any vestiges of slavery which may remain in our country.' *This is theory.* In *practice*, they urge the lower judicatures to prepare the young slaves 'for the exercise of liberty *when God*, in his providence, *shall open a door for emancipation.*' This recommendation is an implied permission to their slave-holding members to dismiss all thoughts of emancipation *at present*, waiting for some colonization opening, or some undefined providence of God." In 1816 the General Assembly allude to slavery as "a mournful evil"; but at the same time they discreetly *erase their note to the eighth commandment*, in which, in 1794, they had stigmatized slave-holding as "man-stealing."

In 1818 this General Assembly, under a somewhat notable impulse of moral courage, issued an "expression of views," in which slavery is called "a gross violation of the most precious and sacred rights of human nature, utterly inconsistent with the law of God, which requires us to love our neighbor as ourselves, and totally irreconcilable with the spirit and principles of the Gospel of Christ, which enjoins that all things whatsoever ye would that men should do to you, do ye also to them."

This was a promising commencement; but how "lame and impotent" the "conclusion"! "Instead of requiring the instant abandonment of this gross violation of rights, &c., the Assembly exhorts the violators to 'continue and increase their exertions to effect a total abolition of slavery, with *no greater delay* than a regard to the *public welfare* demands'!"* Here observe, the persons who are convicted of "a gross violation of the most precious and sacred rights of human nature," are gravely advised to "increase their exertions" to cease from their sin, "with no greater delay than a regard for the public welfare demands"! How long the public welfare may require a persistence in this "gross violation" of human rights, the Assembly does not presume to decide.

It proceeds, however, to recommend that, "if a Christian professor shall sell a slave who is also in communion with our Church," without the slave's *consent*, he "should be suspended till he should repent and make reparation"! † Observe here that no penalty is annexed to the selling of a slave, even though "in communion with our Church," if the slave makes no objection; and if the slave be *not* "in communion with our Church," he may be sold, willing or unwilling, and the dealer in human flesh incur not even ecclesiastical censure!

In order to see what effect this "expression of views" had in mitigating the cruelties of slavery, we have only to look into a "Report" on the subject adopted by the Synod of Kentucky in 1834. Alluding to the horrors of the domestic slave-trade, and to the forcible separation of families, the Report says: —

"These acts are daily occurring in the midst of us." "There is not a village or road that does not

* Goodell. American Churches, &c., by J. G. Birney.
† Birney's American Churches.

behold the sad procession of manacled outcasts, whose chains and mournful countenances tell that they are exiled by force from all that their hearts hold dear. Our Church, years ago, raised its voice of solemn warning against this *flagrant violation of every principle of mercy, justice, and humanity.* Yet we blush to announce to you that this warning has been often disregarded, even by those who hold to our communion. Cases have occurred in our own denomination where *professors of the religion of mercy* HAVE TORN THE MOTHER FROM THE CHILDREN, *and sent her into a merciless and returnless exile.* Yet acts of discipline have rarely followed such conduct."

One would naturally suppose that the knowledge of such terrible crimes, committed in the very bosom of the Church, would have stimulated measures leading to some reform; but nothing of the kind took place. Mr. Birney, formerly a resident of Kentucky, assures us that no act of discipline was ever applied to such offences. The Synod of Kentucky, with the fullest knowledge of these dreadful facts, have remained opposed to the immediate abolition of slavery; and the only minister within their limits who ventured to propose unconditional emancipation was banished from their edifying society.

In 1835, a ruling elder in this Church, MR. STEWART of Illinois, in urging some anti-slavery action upon the General Assembly, said: "In this Church a man may take a freeborn child, force it away from its parents, to whom God gave it in charge, saying, 'Bring it up for me,' and sell it as a beast, or hold it in perpetual bondage, and *not only escape corporal punishment, but really be esteemed an excellent Christian.* Nay, even ministers of the Gospel and Doctors of Divinity may engage in this unholy traffic, and yet sustain their high and holy calling." "Elders, ministers, and Doctors of Divinity are, with both hands, engaged in the practice!" *

Will it be credited, that, while no one ventured to call in question the facts here stated, the actors were neither punished, nor was anything done to abate these monstrous offences! On the contrary, from that day the sentiment of the Church became, if possible, more depraved. From a *toleration* of the system involving these odious crimes, the Church lapsed into an open *defence* of slaveholding, and perverted the Bible in its scandalous zeal for this great iniquity.

After the division of the General Assembly in 1838, both the Old School and the New remained faithful to the slave-holders. This is demonstrated by the fact that, so late as 1850, the New School "unanimously" declared itself, "before God and the world," "ready to commune with the Old School,† at a time when the great body of Old-School Presbyterians at the South were zealous for the extension of slavery, demanded of the

* Quoted on the authority of William Goodell, p. 153.

† New York Observer, June 15, 1850.

Federal Government its extension as an act of justice, and defended it as a Bible institution." *

We pass on to the ORTHODOX CONGREGATIONALIST CHURCHES. Although this denomination has furnished several brilliant and earnest opponents of slavery, and although our late political reaction was greatly stimulated by the influence of both its clergy and laity, its general tendency has been in the direction of subserviency and compromise. Its affinity for the Presbyterian Church, and the familiar intercourse subsisting between the two sects, indicate that their feelings have not been very dissimilar as regards the subject under consideration. We had collected considerable documentary evidence showing the guarded and equivocal language in which Congregationalists have been accustomed to allude to this "delicate subject," but we have not space to admit the citations. The well-known pro-slavery views of PROFESSOR STUART of Andover, of DR. WOODS, DR. DANA, and others, and the notorious fact that the Fugitive-Slave Bill had many zealous advocates among Congregationalists, serve to show that the influence of this branch of our ecclesiasticism has been exerted in favor of slavery, rather than against it.

No denomination has gone farther in the defence of slave-holding than the BAPTIST. In rela-

* Goodell, p. 161.

tion to the views of Southern Baptists, let the following sentences testify, extracted from a memorial of the Charleston Baptist Association to the Legislature of South Carolina, in 1835: "The said Association does not consider that the Holy Scriptures have made the fact of slavery a question of morals at all. The Divine Author of our holy religion, in particular, found slavery a part of the existing institutions of society, with which, if not sinful, it was not his design to intermeddle, but to leave them entirely to the control of men. Adopting it, therefore, as one of the allowed relations of society, he made it the province of his religion only to prescribe the reciprocal duties of the relation. The question, it is believed, is purely one of political economy," etc. The Association proceeds to claim for South Carolina the right to "regulate the existence and continuance of slavery within her territorial limits," and adds: "We would resist to the utmost every invasion of this right, come from what quarter and under whatever pretence it may."

How many ages would it require to procure the peaceful abolition of slavery, in a State where the Christian religion is thus invoked to protect it as one of the natural institutions of society, and where the churches themselves are pledged to resist every invasion whatsoever of the alleged right? And in what way could "the providence of God open a door for emancipation," among such a people, except through the horrors of a servile insurrection, or by the mandate of Federal authority?

In 1833, the REV. DR. FURMAN edified the Governor of South Carolina with an exposition of the "Views of Baptists" on the peculiar institution, in which he said: "The right of holding slaves is clearly established in the Holy Scriptures, both by precept and example." The precept and example of this reverend Doctor certainly coincided, for when his effects came to be advertised for sale, on his decease, among the articles enumerated were "TWENTY-SEVEN NEGROES, some of them very prime."

How far the Baptists of the North are responsible for such sentiments will appear by the following remark, made in 1834, by the late REV. LUCIUS BOLLES, D. D., of Massachusetts, Corresponding Secretary of the American Baptist Board for Foreign Missions: "There is a *pleasing degree of union* among the multiplying thousands of Baptists *throughout the land*. . . . . . Our Southern brethren are generally, both ministers and people, slave-holders."* Such were the people who, deliberately fostering the most dreadful condition of heathenism at home, made a merit of preaching their pro-slavery religion to the heathen abroad.

We must hasten through these scandalous records. The prevailing course of the PROTESTANT EPISCOPAL CHURCH, with respect to slavery, has

* Birney's American Churches.

been indicated by JOHN JAY, ESQ. (himself an Episcopalian), in a pamphlet entitled "Thoughts on the Duty of the Episcopal Church," &c. "She has," observes MR. JAY, "not merely remained a mute and careless spectator of this great conflict of truth and justice with hypocrisy and cruelty, but her very priests and deacons may be seen ministering at the altar of slavery,—offering their talents and influence at its unholy shrine, and openly repeating the awful blasphemy, that the precepts of our Saviour sanction the system of American slavery. Her Northern (free State) clergy, with rare exceptions, whatever they may feel on the subject, rebuke it neither in public nor in private; and her periodicals, far from advancing the progress of abolition, at times oppose our societies, impliedly defending slavery, as not incompatible with Christianity, and occasionally withholding information useful to the cause of freedom." *

"In 1836, a clergyman of North Carolina, of the name of FREEMAN, preached in presence of his bishop (REV. LEVI S. IVES, D. D., a native of a free State) two sermons, on the rights and duties of slave-holders. In these he essayed to *justify*, from the Bible, *the slavery of both white men and negroes*, and insisted that, 'without a new revelation from Heaven, no man was authorized to pronounce slavery wrong.' The two sermons were printed in a pamphlet, prefaced with a letter to MR. FREEMAN

* Birney's American Churches, pp. 39, 40.

from the Bishop of North Carolina, declaring that he 'had listened *with most unfeigned pleasure'* to his discourses, and advised their publication as being 'urgently called for at the present time.'"

The position of the ROMAN CATHOLIC CHURCH in this country, on the subject of slavery, is no more honorable than that of the sects we have mentioned. Its general practice has been to *ignore* our national sin at the North, and to *sanction* the practice of slaveholding among its members at the South. DR. O. A. BROWNSON — hitherto known as an apologist for slavery — has recently published an able argument for immediate emancipation;* but we notice that the *New York Metropolitan*, which is understood to be the organ of ARCHBISHOP HUGHES, repudiates the sentiments of MR. BROWNSON, and reiterates some of the stalest charges that have been made against the Abolitionists.

Among UNIVERSALISTS and UNITARIANS there has been, we incline to believe, a stronger anti-slavery sentiment, and a more general agitation of the great question, than among the older sects. This may be due, in part, to the fact that these denominations have few churches located at the South, and also to the more vital spiritual life which is apt to distinguish the more recent religious organizations. Some of the ablest advocates of emanci-

* Birney, p. 41.

† Brownson's Quarterly Review, Oct., 1861.

pation belong to these sects; and their various ecclesiastical bodies have adopted, on different occasions, resolutions strongly condemnatory of the sin of slavery. Still, we question whether the influence of the two denominations, in the aggregate, has been hostile to the great sin of the Republic. We rather fear that, like the older sects, they have done more to countenance the pro-slavery policy of the country, than to create a regenerating public opinion.

As regards the action of the smaller and less influential sects on the subject, we are not so accurately informed. The QUAKERS are popularly reputed an anti-slavery sect, but it is a debatable point how far they are entitled to the merit.

In reviewing the attitude of the Churches at large toward this vitally important issue, the conclusion is depressing in the extreme. To reflect that, in the most momentous debate ever raised in the mind of a Christian nation, the Church actually arrayed herself on the side of oppression and barbarism, ignoring the dictates of justice and suppressing the instincts of piety, turning her back to the claims of freedom, and making herself deaf to the cry of the poor and needy, presents a moral and mental anomaly that may well distress the saint and perplex the philosopher.

DR. ALBERT BARNES, a man whose judgment

is entitled to respect, said: "There is no power *out* of the Church that could sustain slavery an hour, if it were not sustained *in* it." This confession justifies all that the radical Abolitionists have charged, in their familiar assertion that the American Church has become the bulwark of American slavery. We do not forget, of course, that there were some faithful witnesses in all the Churches, during those dark days of ecclesiastical infidelity; or that the pious abhorrence of slavery which had characterized HOPKINS and EDWARDS and WESLEY was ever entirely suppressed. We speak of the general influence and tendency of the Church, as evinced in its ecclesiastical decisions, in the failure of its discipline to take cognizance of the glaring iniquities of slave-holding, and in its efforts to discourage that free discussion of the subject, which alone could lead to a peaceful abrogation of the wrong. In all these respects, the guilt of the Church stands forth in fearful prominence, and we know of no consideration that can essentially palliate it. We have reproduced these odious facts with reluctance and pain, out of no desire to damage the Church, but because a *greater interest* than the welfare of the Church appeared to demand it,—the interest of our country and of humanity, to which our ecclesiastical orders have been notoriously unfaithful.

"Just God, and holy!
Is that Church which lends
Strength to the spoiler, Thine?"

VII.

APPARENT TRIUMPH OF THE DESPOTIC SYSTEM.

THE subjugation of the Church may be esteemed the crowning evidence of the submission of the country to the DESPOTIC SYSTEM. By gradual stages at the beginning, by monstrous strides of aggression in later years, the alien principle now appeared supreme.

Since the acquisition of Missouri it had scarcely affected to disguise its purposes. Its native impudence sprouted luxuriantly in the broad sun of Federal patronage. The manners of the plantation despot began to be transferred to the floor of Congress. Virgin States, each of them ample enough for an empire, were transferred from the aboriginal freemen, and laid at the feet of the hungry despotism. Under the genial leadership of CALHOUN, and in the name of the specious sophism of "State Rights," the latent insubordination of the oligarchy to the supreme law of the land was proclaimed in South Carolina. The endless perpetuity of slavery was announced by HENRY CLAY. The Church was cowed into the decision that pronounced slavery a divine institution, and solemnly consecrated its crimes.

Since slavery was to be perpetual, and since it had become divine, it was time to make it a national institution. By an act of Congress, accordingly, the entire free North was made a hunting-ground for the recovery of fugitives. The old Missouri landmark was blotted out, that the petted system might spread into the Northwest. The domestic slave-trade, in some of its features more revolting than the foreign traffic, had been under the patronage, and within the control, of the Federal Government, almost from the beginning.* MR. BUCHANAN was carried into the Presidency, sworn and consecrated to the pro-slavery policy to crown the culminating succession of executive baseness. The Supreme Court, as we have seen, breaking over all legal precedents and perverting our most glorious traditions, undertook to legalize the tenure of property in man, in every part of the Republic.

Can it be esteemed surprising that sagacious men began to inquire — in view of the general apostasy of the nation — whether God reigns in this world, or the Devil? But the wisest men became reassured. They saw that Divine causes were operating in the land that must eventuate in Divine effects, — that the laws ordained by Eternal Justice, and running through the nature of

* See Goodell, pp. 243-262. Compare Jay's "Inquiry," Part II. Chap. V.

man and the polity of states, cannot be permanently resisted, but vindicate themselves even through the very folly and depravity that would override them.

PART III.

OUR POLITICAL REGENERATION.

"We have offended, O my countrymen!
We have offended very grievously,
And been most tyrannous. From east to west,
A groan of accusation pierces Heaven!
The wretched plead against us; multitudes,
Countless and vehement, the sons of God,
Our brethren!"

COLERIDGE.

"It is not madness
That I have uttered. . . . . For love of grace
Lay not that flattering unction to your soul,
That not your trespass, but my madness speaks:
It will but skin and film the ulcerous place;
While rank corruption, mining all within,
Infects unseen. Confess yourself to Heaven;
Repent what 's past; avoid what is to come;
And do not spread the compost on the weeds,
To make them ranker."

HAMLET.

"O Truth! O Freedom! how are ye still born
In the rude stable, in the manger nursed!
What humble hands unbar those gates of morn,
Through which the splendors of the new day burst!

. . . . . .

"O small beginnings, ye are great and strong,
Based on a faithful heart and weariless brain;
Ye build the future fair, ye conquer wrong,
Ye earn the crown, and wear it not in vain!"

JAMES RUSSELL LOWELL.

"It is not possible for the people of Rome to be slaves, whom the gods have destined to the command of all nations. Other nations may endure slavery, but the proper end and business of the Roman people is liberty." — CICERO.

"Among our politicians are men who regard public life as a charmed circle into which moral principle must not enter, who know no law but expediency, who are prepared to kiss the feet of the South for Southern votes, and who stand ready to echo all the vituperations of the slave-holder against the active enemies of slavery in the free States." — CHANNING.

I.

THE DAWN OF REFORM.

WHILE the despotic principle, with rapacious insolence, was aggressing upon the heritage of freedom; while — emboldened by past success, and gorged with Federal patronage — it was apparently in the act of completing the subjugation of the republic, — a spirit of RESISTANCE, grounded in the moral nature of the best men, and sharpened by discussion and adversity, — despised at first, but continually augmenting in power and in fame, — was rising in the national heart, quickening the national conscience, and preparing to cope with the hitherto resistless apostasy.

The germ of this reform spirit may be traced back to the agitation attending the admission of Missouri. The popular interest in that transaction had been intense. From the floor of Congress, where the rival interests were struggling in the throes of debate, to the backwoods of Arkansas and the Mexican Gulf, on the South, to the frontiers of Maine and the prairies of Illinois, on the North, the storm of agitation swept the land. Many freemen at the North, at that early period, clearly discerned the purposes of the slave Propaganda; apprehended the momentous issue that was preparing for the future; and, as stout-hearted champions of justice, placed their lances in rest for a life-long encounter with the advancing despotism. Reviled and misjudged, persecuted and counter-worked, by those who should have joined hands with them in the great contest, many of those early opponents of slavery became the *salt* of whatever free sentiment survived in America, — A SAVOR OF LIFE to a nation all but mortally corrupted; and their record is yet to be written, their fidelity blazoned, and their principles justified, by a people ransomed through their long-suffering heroism.

One of the earliest and ablest of those who took the field, to resist the formidable advance of the slave power, and to plead for the trampled rights of its victims, was BENJAMIN LUNDY, who established a monthly periodical, the *Genius of Universal Emancipation*, in the year 1821. With the most self-denying and enlightened zeal, MR. LUNDY, in the course of the next ten years, visited nineteen States of the Union, penetrated into Mexico, and performed two voyages to the West Indies, — having held during the period more than two hundred public meetings, travelled upwards of five thousand miles on foot, and sacrificed several thousand dollars of his own hard earnings. To his indefatigable research, the North owes the first disclosure of the Texas plot; and to him belongs the credit of having armed with authentic facts, and inspired with salutary alarm, such men as JOHN QUINCY ADAMS and DR. CHANNING, — the latter of whom confesses, in his letter to HENRY CLAY, his indebtedness to MR. LUNDY's labors.

WILLIAM LLOYD GARRISON became first known to the public, while a journeyman printer at Newburyport, Massachusetts, by paragraphs furnished to the newspaper on which he was employed. Invited to Boston, in 1827 or 1828, to take temporary charge of the only temperance paper then published in the country, he extended his fame. He became first known as an antagonist of slavery, we believe, while editing the *Journal of the Times*, in Vermont.

In 1829, he became associated for a short time with BENJAMIN LUNDY, at Baltimore, in the publication of the *Genius of Universal Emancipation.* This connection led to one of the many remarkable episodes in the history of the Abolition movement. It happened that, about the time of MR. GARRISON'S removal to Baltimore, the ship *Francis*, owned by FRANCIS TODD, of Newburyport, Massachusetts, "being at Baltimore for freight, was employed in taking from thence a cargo of slaves for New Orleans." MR. GARRISON made, in his paper, so severe an allusion to the circumstance, "that MR. TODD directed a suit to be brought against him for a libel." Tried by a Maryland court, in February, 1830, he was convicted in a fine of one hundred dollars, besides costs, and thrown into jail for non-payment of the same. From this conviction sprung the charge, with which some of his opponents were wont to stigmatize him in subsequent years, of his being a "convicted felon." His treatment roused a strong excitement at the North, and gave an impulse to the anti-slavery cause which later events have only accelerated. MR. GARRISON lay in jail about fifty days, when his release was effected, chiefly through the generosity of a New York merchant, MR. ARTHUR TAPPAN, whose name thenceforward, with that of his brother, LEWIS TAPPAN, was identified with the cause of freedom.

In January, 1831, MR. GARRISON, having dissolved partnership with MR. LUNDY, commenced the publication of *The Liberator* in Boston, becoming from that time the stanch standard-bearer in the cause for which he had already suffered.

In an early issue of his new paper he recorded this memorable declaration: "I am aware that many object to the severity of my language; but is there not cause for severity? I *will* be as harsh as truth, and as uncompromising as justice. I am in EARNEST; I will not equivocate; I will not excuse; I will not retreat a single inch; AND I WILL BE HEARD." How nobly the brave man has redeemed his pledge may be seen in the influence which his inflexible genius has exerted during the past thirty years of American history.

The rise of the Abolition Party demonstrated, as

nothing else had ever done, the dangerous ascendency which slavery had already obtained over the nation. The voice of Liberty had already become forgotten. When it swelled again on the air, the people mistook it for the voice of anarchy. It was like proclaiming a new Gospel in a land which had lapsed into Heathenism. The idols were restored; the true God was forgotten. The priests of Baal had supplanted the holy prophets. The very principles recognized by the past generation as "self-evident truths" exasperated their degenerate children. The avowal of Abolitionism — which BENJAMIN FRANKLIN, THOMAS JEFFERSON, JAMES MADISON, JOHN JAY, ALEXANDER HAMILTON, and many of their contemporaries, had gloried in proclaiming — now served, in 1830, to cover with odium the most spotless of men. The very doctrines which had been held by the author of the Declaration, by most of the framers of the Constitution, by Presidents of Colleges, by Governors of States, by Judges in the Federal Courts, by foreign Ministers, by the early Presidents of the United States, and by all the Christian denominations, at the close of the last century, only thirty-five years later subjected men and women to the violence of mobs, to the destruction of their property, and to brutal assassination!

What more conclusive evidence could we require of the *necessity* of a political reformation than that presented in the outrages with which the doctrines of liberty were repelled, and in the strange torpor with which the community saw its noblest champions struck down in the exercise of their inalienable rights?

Dr. Channing, who controverted the position of the Abolitionists, bears generous testimony to the services they rendered, in that critical hour, to the cause of free speech and a free press. "I am myself," he says, "their debtor. I am not sure that I should this moment write in safety had they shrunk from the conflict, — had they shut their lips, imposed silence on their presses, and hid themselves before their ferocious assailants. I know not where these outrages would have stopped had they not met resistance from their first destined victims. The newspaper press, with a few exceptions, uttered no genuine indignant rebuke of the wrong-doers, but rather countenanced, by its gentle censures, the reign of Force. The mass of the people looked supinely on this new tyranny, under which a portion of their fellow-citizens seemed to be sinking. *A tone of denunciation was beginning to proscribe all discussion of slavery;* and had the spirit of violence, which selected associations as its first objects, succeeded in this preparatory enterprise, it might have been easily turned against any and every individual who might presume to agitate the unwelcome subject. . . . . . I thank the Abolitionists that, in this evil day, they were true to the rights which the multitude were ready to betray." *

* Channing's Works, Vol. II. p. 160.

II.

WHY THE REFORM WAS RESISTED.

SOME efforts were made to justify the outrages of the period by charging upon the Abolitionists the most nefarious designs. They intended to instigate servile insurrections. They wanted the slaves to murder their masters. They advocated amalgamation. They were infidels to the Church of Christ, and traitors to the government of their country. All these charges are now known to have been false. Few candid men, having anything like extensive information, ever believed them. They were fabricated in the same base spirit that animated the mobs they were designed to excuse, and that perpetrated the crimes they were designed to shelter from justice. "Who are the men," wrote DR. CHANNING, "whose offences are so aggravated, that they must be denied the protection of the laws, and given up to the worst passions of the multitude? Are they profligate in principle and life, teachers of impious or servile doctrines, the enemies of God and their race? I speak not from vague rumor, but from better means of knowledge, when I say, that a body of men and women more blameless than the Abolitionists in their various relations, or more disposed to adopt a rigid construction of the Christian precepts, cannot be found among us. Of their judiciousness and wisdom, I do not speak, but I believe they yield to no party in moral worth. Their great crime, and one which in this land of liberty is to be punished above all crimes, is this, that they carry the doctrine of human equality to its full extent, that they plead vehemently for the oppressed, that they assail wrong-doing, however sanctioned by opinion or intrenched behind wealth and power, that their zeal for human rights is without measure, that they associate themselves fervently with the Christians and philanthropists of other countries against the worst relic of barbarous times. Such is the offence against which mobs are arrayed, and which is counted so flagrant, that a summary justice too indignant to wait for the tardy progress of tribunals must take the punishment into its own hands." *

In his essay on "Slavery," DR. CHANNING thus refers to this body of reformers, "everywhere spoken against": "As a party, they are singularly free from political and religious sectarianism, and have been distinguished by the absence of management, calculation, and worldly wisdom. That they have ever proposed or desired insurrection or violence among the slaves, there is no reason to believe. All their principles repel the

* Channing's Works, Vol. II. p. 162.

supposition. It is a remarkable fact, that though the South and the North have been leagued to crush them, though they have been watched by a million of eyes, and though prejudice has been prepared to detect the slightest sign of corrupt communication with the slave, yet this crime has not been fastened on a single member of this body." *

The real offence of the Abolitionists consisted, beyond question, in the soundness of their principles and the veracity of their statements. Said the sagacious old Fuller, "I should suspect that his preaching had no salt in it, if no galled horse did wince." The Church leaders and the politicians were the galled horses of that era, and the pungent TRUTHS which the reformers showered upon the community were the *salt* that set them bounding with indignation.

* Works, Vol. II. p. 124.

III.

THE VANGUARD OF LIBERTY.

At the outset, the Abolitionists — themselves devoted members of different churches and parties — counted on being able to enlist the religious and political organizations of the North in the cause of emancipation. Mr. William Goodell relates that he accompanied Mr. Garrison, in 1829, in calling upon a number of prominent ministers in Boston, to secure their co-operation in the cause, their expectations of important assistance from the clergy being at that time very sanguine.

In his address before the Colonization Society, delivered in the Park Street Church, Boston, on the 4th of July, 1829, Mr. Garrison had said: "I call on the ambassadors of Christ everywhere to make known this proclamation: 'Thus saith the Lord God of the Africans, Let this people go, that they may serve me.' I ask them to 'proclaim liberty to the captive, and the opening of the prison to them that are bound.' I call on the churches of the living God to LEAD in this great enterprise." But the ministers withheld their influence; the church doors were closed against those apostles of freedom; and the ecclesiastical polity of the country, locking hands with the perverted civil government, endeavored to resist the progress of the reform.

At that time, the REV. DR. LYMAN BEECHER, in the meridian of his fame, and the acknowledged leader of New England orthodoxy, was "the bright particular star" of the Boston pulpit. MR. GARRISON had been one of those who bowed to the spell of that preacher's eloquence, and hailed him as one of the mightiest of God's witnesses. "He waited on his favorite divine, and urged him to give to the new movement the incalculable aid of his name and countenance. He was patiently heard. He was allowed to unfold his plans and array his facts. The reply of the veteran was: 'MR. GARRISON, I have too many irons in the fire to put in another.'" The ardent reformer responded: "Doctor, you had better take them all out and put this one in, if you mean well either to the religion or to the civil liberty of our country." *

The illustrious but maligned leader of the Abolitionists speaks as follows of their position, their motives, and their aims: "Originally they were generally members of the various religious bodies, tenacious of their theological views, full of veneration for the organized Church and ministry, but ignorant of the position in which these stood to the 'sum of all villanies.' What would ulti-

* Stated on the authority of Wendell Phillips.

mately be required of them by a faithful adherence to the cause of the slave, in their church relations, their political connections, their social ties, their worldly interest and reputation, they knew not. Instead of seeking a controversy with the pulpit and the Church, they confidently looked to both for efficient aid to their cause. Instead of suddenly withdrawing from the pro-slavery religious and political organizations with which they were connected, they lingered long and labored hard to bring them to repentance. They were earnest, but well-balanced; intrepid, but circumspect; importunate, but long-suffering. Their controversy was neither personal nor sectional; their object neither to arraign any sect nor to assail any party primarily. They sought to liberate the slave by every righteous instrumentality, and nothing more. But, to their grief and amazement, they were gradually led to perceive, by the terrible revelations of the hour, that the religious forces on which they had relied were all arrayed on the side of the oppressor, that the North was as hostile to emancipation as the South, that the spirit of slavery was omnipresent, invading every sanctuary, infecting every pulpit, controlling every press, corrupting every household, and blinding every vision; that no other alternative was presented to them, except to wage war with 'principalities and powers and spiritual wickedness in high places,' and to separate themselves from every slave-holding alliance; or else to substitute compromise for principle, and thus betray the rights and liberties of the millions in thraldom, at a fearful cost to their own souls. If some of them faltered and perished by the way, if others deserted the cause and became its bitterest enemies, if others still withdrew from the ranks, their sectarian attachment overmastering their love of humanity, and leading them basely to misrepresent and revile their old associates, the main body proved fearless and incorruptible; and, through the American Anti-Slavery Society and its auxiliaries, have remained steadfast to the present hour."*

From the commencement of the *Liberator*, in 1831, to the establishment of the right of petition, in 1845, the Abolitionists fought the battle of liberty against a degenerate age, with an intrepidity and persistence, with a fidelity and heroism, that find no parallel on this continent. Theirs became a contest, not simply in behalf of the freedom of the colored race, but also in behalf of the right of the American people to free speech and a free press, — a right which, but for their dignified and resolute resistance, might have been yielded up at the demand of the Southern despots and their pliant retainers. At the cost of fourteen years' effort and suffering, by tireless research, debate, expostulation, and petition, in the face of igno-

* See an anti-slavery tract entitled "The 'Infidelity' of Abolitionism," p. 7.

rance and bigotry, of partisan malice and fanatical violence, that band of iron men and loyal women RESCUED THE NATION from the clutch of the slave power, displayed the resistless energy of truth, and vindicated for all time, let us trust, the benefit of free inquiry and fair discussion.

Let us notice some of their measures, and a few of the wrongs they were called to suffer.

IV.

ORGANIZATION AND OPPOSITION.

In January, 1832, the New England Anti-Slavery Society was organized in Boston, and, with meagre resources, went into operation. *The New York Evangelist* espoused the cause, and contributed to augment the discussion. *The Genius of Temperance* was already enlisted on the side of freedom. Both these papers enjoyed an extensive circulation at that time in most of the States, South as well as North. In the spring of 1833, by the liberality of Arthur and Lewis Tappan, merchants of New York, *The Emancipator* was commenced. During the same year, partly through the same generous instrumentality, large numbers of anti-slavery tracts were issued, and sent by mail to the clergy of all denominations, and to prominent men, throughout the country. By these means, the discussion of slavery became inaugurated in most of the free States. It roused the people from their lethargy, and compelled them to take sides. And, although the majority were alarmed, and followed the bent of their prejudices, or the beck of their party and sectarian leaders, instead of candidly examining the merits of the cause, many powerful men were enlisted at that period.*

The doctrine of the Abolitionists, that of immediate and unconditional emancipation on the soil, brought them in collision, not only with the general prejudice of the time, but with the Colonization Society in particular.

This Society had been formed about the year 1816, at the suggestion of the Virginia Legislature, and solely through the agency of slave-holders. Its object, as defined by its own constitution, was "to promote and execute a plan for colonizing (with their consent) the free people of color residing in our country, in Africa, or such other place as Congress shall deem most expedient."† The grand aim of the Society, as disclosed by its subsequent proceedings, was to induce the General and State governments to provide means for the removal of the free Negroes from their midst, thereby reducing the chances of servile insurrections; and at the same time to furnish a plausible occasion for the humane sentiment of the country to vent itself without damage to the system of slavery. It was a device every way worthy of the profound craft of the slave-holding oligarchy; and it imposed upon thousands of people at the North, who flattered themselves that they were doing something to mitigate the sufferings of the colored race,

* Goodell, pp. 392, 393.

† See Constitution of the Society, Art. 11.

whereas they were really contributing to perpetuate their wrongs.*

The Abolitionists boldly exposed the fraudulent pretences with which the claims of the Colonization Society were advocated at the North, having received in their own persons, from members of that Society, abundant evidence of its hostility to any scheme of emancipation. And their views were ultimately confirmed in a celebrated speech of HENRY CLAY, himself one of the authors of the colonization scheme, in which he announced his conviction that slavery must be perpetual, though the African race would perish under the system. That startling declaration of MR. CLAY opened the eyes of many Northern people. They saw that, if the great Kentuckian had given utterance to the real sentiment of the South, there was no alternative between radical Abolitionism and the endless perpetuity of that dreadful system which was to extinguish the black race and engulf the white.

On the 2d of October, 1833, a New York City Anti-Slavery Society was formed, the event being signalized "by demonstrations of tumult and violence." The meeting had been called at Clinton Hall, but, inasmuch as a counter notice, signed by "Many Southrons," called a meeting at the same time and place, the Abolitionists assembled at Chatham Street Chapel. "Their opposers, find-

* Goodell, pp. 342 – 352. See also "An Inquiry into the Character and Tendency of the American Colonization and American Anti-Slavery Societies."

ing Clinton Hall closed, adjourned to Tammany Hall, and made speeches and adopted resolutions against them." Learning, at length, where the Abolitionists were assembled, they adjourned by acclamation, and poured into the Chatham Street Chapel with the avowed purpose of "routing" its peaceful occupants. The meeting had already adjourned, but most of the attendants were still in the house. The rioters called for several Abolitionists by name, and the words, "Ten thousand dollars for ARTHUR TAPPAN!" were shouted by the mob. No personal violence, however, was done.

The mob-meeting at Tammany Hall had been "organized by prominent citizens, addressed by popular public speakers," and it was commended by the city press. "By the same class of citizens a colonization meeting was promptly called. . . . . . The Mayor of the city presided. The orators dwelt on the reckless agitations of the Abolitionists. Not a word of disapprobation of the late outrage against them was uttered. THEODORE FRELINGHUYSEN, United States Senator from New Jersey, charged them with 'seeking to dissolve the Union.' CHANCELLOR WALWORTH was in attendance, from Albany, to declare their efforts 'unconstitutional,' and to denounce them as 'reckless incendiaries.' DAVID B. OGDEN, ESQ., declared 'the doctrine of immediate emancipation a direct and palpable nullification of the Constitution.' MR. FRELINGHUYSEN further declared, that 'nine tenths of the horrors of slavery are imaginary,' and 'the crusade of abolition' he regarded as 'the poetry of philanthropy.'" *

Still, the reform grew. In December, 1833, a National Anti-Slavery Convention, represented by delegates from ten States, met at Philadelphia. "BERIAH GREEN, President of Oneida Institute, was chosen President of the Convention, and LEWIS TAPPAN and JOHN G. WHITTIER, Secretaries. The members united in signing a declaration of their sentiments, objects, and measures, prepared in committee, from a draft by MR. GARRISON. This Convention organized the American Anti-Slavery Society. . . . . . The Executive Committee was located in New York City, the seat of the Society's operations, which were now prosecuted with vigor. *The Emancipator*, under the editorial charge of WILLIAM GOODELL, one of the Executive Committee, became the organ of the Society. Tracts, pamphlets, and books were published and circulated, a large number of lecturing agents were employed, conventions were held," and auxiliary societies organized throughout the free States.†

In this way was carried forward the great reform which first broke the despotism of the slave power at the North, and which has inspired and equipped all subsequent movements tending to our political regeneration.

* Goodell, pp. 395, 396.

† Ibid., pp. 396, 397.

V.

THE OPPOSITION BY MOBS.

THE progress of the work roused a resistance every way characteristic of the gigantic evil that was to be overthrown. "An attempt to hold an anti-slavery meeting in the city of New York, on the 4th of July, 1834, was made the occasion of a frightful and protracted riot. The meeting was broken up, and for several successive days and evenings the city was in possession of the rioters, who assaulted private dwellings and places of public worship, and attempted personal violence upon Abolitionists. Similar scenes were enacted in Philadelphia, a few weeks afterwards. Extensive damages were done to the private dwellings and public buildings of the unoffending colored people, who had been cruelly maligned, and wantonly held up to public odium, at a Colonization meeting a short time previous. During these riots, which were of several days' recurrence, many of the colored people were wounded, and some of them lost their lives. These early examples of lawlessness — notoriously countenanced, as they were, by men of wealth and influence, excited by eloquent orators, and palliated afterwards by the public press — furnished precedents for similar outrages throughout the free States for a series of years."

We can but glance at two or three of these disgraceful events. At Canaan, New Hampshire, on the 10th of August, 1835, an academy was demolished by a mob, because colored youth were admitted to its privileges.

At Boston, on the 21st of October, the Female Anti-Slavery Society was dispersed while the President was at prayer. The mob engaged in this chivalrous enterprise was composed of five thousand "gentlemen of property and standing," as they were described by the city press. Finding MR. GARRISON in the street, they seized him, and dragged him some distance with a rope around his body. The Mayor of the city, hardly daring to cross the wishes of this mob of "gentlemen," lodged MR. GARRISON in the jail for protection. Soon after, at the "earnest entreaty" of the city authorities, he left Boston for a brief season. Like certain reformers of old, he "had filled Jerusalem with his doctrine," and the Sanhedrim of Boston were driven to their wits' end to know what to do with him.

At Utica, New York, on the same day, "a member of Congress" headed a committee of "twenty-five prominent citizens" who proceeded to break up "a meeting convened to form a New York State Anti-Slavery Society, and threw down the press of a Democratic journal, which had espoused the anti-slavery cause. By invitation of HON.

GERRIT SMITH, who, on that occasion, identified himself with them, the Abolitionists repaired to his residence at Peterboro', twenty-five miles distant," where they completed their organization. The trinity of outrages which disgraced the memorable day was completed at Montpelier, Vermont, by a demonstration of mob violence against the REV. SAMUEL J. MAY, resulting in the breaking up of a meeting which he had called in that town.

In December, 1836, the Southern students at Yale College, New Haven, broke up an anti-slavery meeting convened in that city. "At Alton, Ill., November 7th, 1837, the press of the Alton *Observer* was destroyed by a mob, and the editor, REV. ELIJAH P. LOVEJOY, shot dead, receiving four balls in his breast. The murderers were not brought to justice."

In Philadelphia, on the 17th of May, 1838, Pennsylvania Hall was burned by a mob, because it had been opened to the obnoxious reformers. At Cincinnati, September 5th, 1841, the printing-press of the *Philanthropist*, edited by JAMES G. BIRNEY (formerly a slave-holder in Kentucky), was destroyed, for the third time, by a ferocious mob.*

Well might DR. CHANNING — one of the most candid spectators of these events — declare, "that our history contains no page more disgraceful to us as freemen, than that which records the violences against the Abolitionists." During all that time,

* Goodell, pp. 404 – 407.

people were being told that men at the North had no concern with slavery, — that the "fanatics" were meddling with a foreign interest; whereas it was a notorious fact, that the despotic system had so far encroached upon the North, and so deplorably corrupted Northern society, that it had become about as dangerous to rebuke it in Boston or New York, in Philadelphia or Cincinnati, as it would have been in Charleston or New Orleans. The lash of the slave-holder was virtually brandished in the face of every man who dared to say that slavery is a sin.

VI.

SUBSERVIENCY OF THE NORTH.

WE have witnessed the first resolute effort to break the authority of the DESPOTIC SYSTEM at the North. We have seen, in the fanatical resistance that was opposed to that peaceful effort, how the cause of the slave's emancipation became identified with the right of a free people to discuss and publish their honest convictions. The advent of Abolitionism revealed the fact, that the Southern despotism had not only subjugated the liberties of the negro, but also encroached to an ominous extent on the prerogatives of the white man. Hence it happened that many discerning persons, who regarded the idea of immediate emancipation as visionary and impracticable, hailed and honored the Abolitionists, nevertheless, as timely and bold asserters of the right of the American citizen to free discussion and a free press.

The alarm and rage which the progress of the reform elicited at the South may be readily apprehended. The system of slavery can be protected only by suppressing discussion. Allow inquiry, research, reflection, and the odious depravity of the system stands revealed, — convicted of being so bad that no consideration can palliate or excuse it. If conscience be quickened, if the sense of justice be allowed to speak, if light fall upon the great wrong, it must disappear. Conscious of these facts, the slave-holders saw in the reviving discussion of the subject at the North the omen of their coming ruin. In the West Indies, too, the process of emancipation, transpiring under the most satisfactory auspices, had already vindicated the most radical plans of reform, and it held out a perpetual invitation to the United States to seek both safety and honor in an act of national justice.

Besides, the agitation of the question was liable to penetrate to the slaves, and stimulate servile insurrections. The affair at Southampton, in Virginia, in 1831, headed by Nat Turner, and the discovery of the slave plot at Charleston a few years earlier, had shown the South that their social system was built over a powder-magazine, and that every family drew breath amid the most awful possibilities.

With the blind wilfulness characteristic of despotism, the slave-holders refused to see that their danger and prospective ruin were the necessary corollaries of their system, — not to be averted by arbitrary efforts to suppress discussion in free States, but to be accepted as the retributive element inseparable from wanton oppression. *Their* attitude toward the reform was at least natural, and the measures they resorted to may be fairly viewed as the simple dictates of their instinct.

The conduct of their abettors at the North was less excusable. The opposition in the free States was dictated by commercial interest, by partisan prejudice, and by sectarian selfishness. Many of the merchants in the large cities enjoyed a lucrative trade with the South, and were virtually under bonds to ignore the abominations of slavery. Both the great political parties of the day were in the power of the South, and bound to do its bidding. This the leaders of those parties well knew, but the masses of the people who supported them were not admitted to the political secrets of the time. The Churches had their Southern connections, and the interests of denominational unity required them to acquiesce in the public opinion that indorsed the slave system.

Thus the whole North was bound to the South by commercial, political, and ecclesiastical ties; and hence a great majority of the Northern people, in the first great issue raised by the Abolitionists, espoused the cause of despotism.

VII.

THE OPPOSITION BY STATES.

SINCE riots and mobs, countenanced by the civil authorities, had proved inadequate to subdue the discussion or arrest the reform, it was proposed to invoke the majesty of the State and Federal Governments. In the Literary and Theological Review for December, 1835, published in the city of New York, the position was elaborately argued, that the "radicals," meaning the Abolitionists, were "*justly liable to the highest civil penalties* and ecclesiastical censures." This sentiment received no rebuke from any of the patrons of the "Review," nor even from the organs of the rival theological party.

In the very spirit of this sentiment, a grand jury of the County of Oneida, just previous to the riot at Utica, made a presentment, in which they declared, that those who form Abolition societies are guilty of sedition, that they ought to be punished, and that it is the duty of all citizens loyal to the Constitution to destroy their publications wherever found.

In the same year, the HON. WILLIAM SULLIVAN issued a pamphlet in Boston, in which the following extraordinary desire is expressed: "It is to be *hoped* and *expected* that Massachusetts will enact laws, declaring the printing, publishing, and circulating papers and pamphlets on slavery, and also the holding of meetings to discuss slavery and abolition, to be public indictable offences, and provide for the punishment thereof in such manner as will more effectually prevent such offences." *

The South was not backward in stimulating such sentiments and measures in the free States. The temper of the South, estimated by the legislative and ecclesiastical memorials of the period, was exceedingly vindictive and ferocious. The native malignity of slavery gushed forth in official acts, reeking with the barbarity of feudal times. The venom of the popular hatred toward the Abolitionists exceeded the darkest annals of Italian rancor, when Italy was most seditious and most depraved. The Southern Church shared the diabolical spirit, and many of her clergy emulated the vindictive passion of the BORGIAS toward their rivals, in their frantic opposition to the idea of emancipation, and their besotted devotion to chattel slavery.

As far back as December, 1831, the Legislature of Georgia, with the approval of GOVERNOR LUMPKIN, passed an act offering five thousand dollars to whoever might arrest and bring to trial, *under the*

* Goodell, pp. 409, 410.

laws of that State, the editor or publisher of *The Liberator*. By the laws of Georgia, MR. GARRISON would have suffered death. But he was not a citizen of that State, and could have been taken there for trial only by an act of felonious abduction, — an act which the Georgia Legislature thus invited and offered to reward. Yet the State of Massachusetts took no notice of the dastardly proposition to kidnap one of her citizens; so base had become the sentiment of that once noble Commonwealth. The example of Georgia was followed at New Orleans, by the offer of twenty thousand dollars for the seizure of ARTHUR TAPPAN. Similar advertisements, specifying prominent Abolitionists, and offering large rewards for their abduction, were extensively circulated by "our Southern brethren"!

With an impudence that posterity will find it hard to credit, the Southern State Legislatures adopted resolutions calling upon the free State governments to enact PENAL LAWS against Abolition societies, and against all efforts to discuss the subject of slavery. But it must astonish the coming age yet more to learn that the Governors of Massachusetts and New York — one a Whig, the other a Democrat — were both disposed to favor these despotic measures.

In the Legislature of Rhode Island, in February, 1836, a bill was actually reported in conformity to the demands of the South.

GOVERNOR GAYLE, of Alabama, went so far as

to demand of GOVERNOR MARCY, of New York, the delivery of R. G. WILLIAMS, publishing agent of the American Anti-Slavery Society, that he might be tried by the laws of Alabama — a State within whose territory he had never been — for having issued in *The Emancipator* a sentiment hostile to slavery. GOVERNOR MARCY declined complying with this extraordinary requisition, but was favorable to the enactment of laws in New York for the punishment of such offences!

In Ohio, in 1838, GOVERNOR VANCE, on requisition of GOVERNOR CLARK, of Kentucky, did deliver up one of its citizens to be tried in the latter State, on an indictment for assisting in the escape of slaves. The person thus arrested — JOHN B. MAHAN, a local minister in the Methodist Episcopal Church — had not been in Kentucky for nineteen years! Yet "he was torn from his family, hurried to Kentucky, and shut up in jail, without allowing him time to procure a writ of *habeas corpus*, or summon evidence in his defence. He was tried at the Circuit Court of Kentucky, in Marion County, the 18th of November. It was admitted by the Attorney for the Commonwealth that the prisoner was a citizen of Ohio, and not in Kentucky at the time of the alleged offence; yet he made an effort to procure his conviction. The jury returned a verdict of not guilty." * Yet it had continually been said, by those who would suppress agitation, that *we* at the North have

* Goodell, pp. 410 – 415, 440.

nothing to do with slavery! Nothing to do with it! when, before the date even of the Fugitive Slave Bill, innocent men were liable to be arrested, or kidnapped, by its emissaries, and dragged before the dubious justice embodied in a Southern court!

VIII.

THE OPPOSITION BY THE FEDERAL POWER.

While the States were agitating the question of suppressing the slavery discussion by statutes, the Federal government—faithful to that uniform policy which had acquired the character of an instinct — arrayed itself on the side of despotism. "The occasion for exerting this influence was presented by the excitement growing out of the transmission of anti-slavery publications through the United States mails. Some of these publications were gratuitously sent, — not to any portion of the colored people, either the free or the enslaved, — but to prominent citizens, statesmen, clergymen, merchants, planters, and professional gentlemen at the South, whose names and residences were known at the North. There could be no reasonable pretence that this measure could excite an insurrection of the slaves. General Duff Green, editor of *The Washington Telegraph*, — one of the most violent opposers of the Abolitionists, — admitted that there was little or no danger of this; and that the real ground of apprehension was, that the publications would 'operate upon the consciences and fears of slave-holders themselves, from the insinuation of their dangerous heresies into our schools, our pulpits, and our domestic circles.' 'It is only,' said he, 'by alarming the consciences of the weak and feeble, and by diffusing among our own people a morbid sensibility on the subject of slavery, that Abolitionists can accomplish their object.'"

On the 29th of July, 1835, a riotous mob broke into the post-office at Charleston, South Carolina, violated the United States mail, and destroyed certain anti-slavery publications found there. From an editorial allusion to the outrage in the *Courier*, it seems that "arrangements had previously been made at the post-office in the city to arrest the circulation of incendiary matter, until instructions could be received from the Post-Office Department at Washington." It would have appeared most expedient, in any law-abiding community, to have waited for the "instructions" before violating the mail. But the people of Charleston were evidently assured that any act they might perpetrate in the interest of slavery, however illegal, would be favorably construed at Washington. The event showed that they were not mistaken. In reply to the application for instructions, the Postmaster-General, AMOS KENDALL, said he was satisfied that he "had no legal authority to exclude newspapers from the mail, nor to prohibit their carriage or delivery on account of their character or tendency, real or supposed." The anti-slavery papers, then, were clearly entitled to be transmitted through the mails. What then? MR. KENDALL continues: "BUT I am not prepared to direct you to forward or deliver the papers of which you speak!" "By no act or direction of mine, official or private, could I be induced to aid, knowingly, in giving circulation to papers of this description," — although he had just confessed that he had no legal authority for excluding them from the mails. "We owe an obligation to the laws," MR. KENDALL proceeds to admit, "but a *higher* one to the communities in which we live; and if the former be permitted to destroy the latter, it is patriotism to disregard them." That is to say, if a law of the United States, which that official was sworn to see executed, threatened to endanger the immunities of slavery, he advised that "a higher obligation" required that it be disregarded! Thus we find the "higher law" actually invoked, in the interest of slavery, against a law of the United States.

Encouraged by the example of the postmaster at Charleston, and by the avowed decision of the Postmaster-General to wink at all similar outrages, other postmasters, North as well as South, lawlessly excluded anti-slavery writings from the mails.

To crown the formidable coalition against the cause of Freedom, PRESIDENT JACKSON, in his annual message (December, 1835), called "the special attention of Congress to the subject," and recommended the passage of a penal law against the circulation of anti-slavery publications in the Southern States.

IX.

FINAL STRUGGLE AND TRIUMPHANT ASSERTION OF FREEDOM IN THE NORTH.

THE most gloomy presages ushered in the winter of 1835–36. It was generally expected that the action recommended by the South to the Northern Legislatures, and by the President to Congress, would be adopted. No remonstrance was uttered, no sign of alarm was expressed, on the part of the Northern community, except by the proscribed and feeble party who were apparently marked for destruction. They, conscious that everything was at stake, girded themselves for a final effort.

The Executive Committee of the American Anti-Slavery Society at New York drew up a solemn protest, involving a thorough review of the charges preferred in the President's Message, and addressed to the Chief Magistrate. In that paper they repelled the charge of insurrectionary designs. "They invited investigation by a Committee of Congress, and offered to submit to their inspection all their publications, all their correspondence, and all their accounts, — promising to attest them, and to answer every question under oath." * The Presi-

* Goodell, p. 417.

dent never noticed this remonstrance; but it is probable that the firm and dignified tone in which it was expressed had its due effect upon the Executive mind. Neither JACKSON nor any of his successors, it is believed, ever repeated the charges contained in his Message, and so boldly met in that protest.

In February, 1836, a Convention met at Providence, for the purpose of forming a Rhode Island Anti-Slavery Society, in response to "a call of respectable citizens in all parts of the State. It was numerously attended, well sustained, and did much to revive the spirit of ROGER WILLIAMS in that part of New England."

The most imposing conflict of the season took place in Massachusetts. A joint committee of both branches of the Legislature, with SENATOR LUNT Chairman, had been appointed to consider the Southern demands. A request of the Abolitionists to enjoy the customary hearing before this committee had received no attention, and it was believed that the committee would report without listening to their defence. "The Anti-Slavery Committee at Boston were at length unexpectedly notified that an audience would be given them the very next day, March 4th, 1836. They hastily rallied, selected their advocates, and prepared for their defence. The interview was held in the Representatives' Hall, neither of the houses being in session, but most of the members of both houses and many prominent citizens being present. After remarks by REV. SAMUEL J. MAY and ELLIS GRAY LORING, ESQ., they were followed by PROFESSOR CHARLES FOLLEN, who, in the course of his remarks, alluded to the recent outrages against Abolitionists, observing that any legislative enactments or censures against the already persecuted party would tend to encourage their assailants and increase their persecutions. Taking offence at this remark, the Chairman, MR. LUNT, silenced PROFESSOR FOLLEN, and abruptly terminated the interview; whereupon the Abolitionists took prompt measures for issuing their suppressed defence in a pamphlet form, which, comprising above forty pages, was prepared for the press in the two following days. A Boston editor, BENJAMIN F. HALLET, ESQ., gave some account of the proceedings, and said the Abolitionists were entitled to a fair hearing. The Legislature directed their committee to allow a completion of the defence, which was accordingly notified for Monday P. M., the 8th instant. The adjacent country was by this time roused, and the Hall of the Representatives was crowded. PROFESSOR FOLLEN concluded his speech, and was followed by SAMUEL E. SEWALL, ESQ., WILLIAM LLOYD GARRISON, and WILLIAM GOODELL, — the latter of whom, instead of making any further defence of Abolitionists, or proving that their publications were not insurrectionary, proceeded to charge upon the Southern States, who had made these demands, a conspiracy against the liberties of the free North. This opened an entire new field. Great uneasiness was manifested by the committee; but the speaker — though repeatedly interrupted by the Chairman — succeeded in quoting the language of GOVERNOR McDUFFIE'S message, and in characterizing the Southern documents lying on the table of the committee before him as being *fetters* for Northern freemen. He had commenced making the inquiry, 'Mr. Chairman, are you prepared to attempt putting them on?' but the sentence was only half finished when the stentorian voice of the Chairman interrupted him: 'Sit down, sir!' — He sat down. The Legislative Committee presently began to move from their seats, but the audience sat petrified with suppressed feeling. The late DR. WILLIAM E. CHANNING was seated among the Abolitionists, though not in form or in sentiment fully identified with them. On such an occasion he could not be absent, and his presence was felt. His countenance seemed to express what words could not have uttered; more eloquent in silence than even he could have been in speech. The Legislative Committee themselves lingered, as in vague expectation. Then rose a respectable merchant of Boston, MR. BOND, unaccustomed, as he said, to public speaking, and begged the committee to wait a few minutes. It was growing dark, and the hall was unlighted, but they sat down. MR. BOND briefly reminded them that freedom of speech and of the press could never be surrendered by the sons of the Pilgrims. He was followed by another volunteer, DR. BRADFORD, from old Plymouth Rock." The committee finally rose, and, with the audience, slowly retired from the room. "A low murmur of voices," sounding through the dim hall, indicated the awakened sympathies of the assembly, and, "like the distant roar of the sea, told of power. Three days afterward, the printed plea of the Abolitionists was on the desk of each member of the Legislature, in the hands of the Governor, and in process of circulation through the Commonwealth. MR. LUNT and his committee delayed their Report till near the close of the session, several weeks later. It was a stale repetition of trite declamation on the subject, but recommending no distinct action by the Legislature." *

Similar attempts in other Northern legislatures to enact laws prohibiting the discussion of slavery likewise failed. The tide was beginning to be effectually turned.

The proposition of PRESIDENT JACKSON to Congress for a prohibitory law was referred to a select committee, of which JOHN C. CALHOUN was Chairman. That committee submitted a Report, February 4, 1836, in which it was maintained that the measure suggested by the President would involve a violation of the Constitution, and an infringement of the liberties of the people, as well as a remote danger to slavery itself. The Report then proceeded to recommend that the STATES be authorized to prohibit the circulation

* Goodell (himself a prominent actor in the scene), pp. 418 – 420.

of such publications as may be "calculated to disturb their security"; and that the Federal postmasters be forbidden to deliver any publications touching the subject of slavery in those States that may prohibit their circulation. A bill, drafted by the committee, in accordance with its own recommendation, was defeated on the final vote.

Here ended the efforts of the slave-holders to instal their despotism over the mails. But the opponents of their project did not rest till they had secured the passage of an act, at the same session, under the signature of the President, prohibiting any such arbitrary measure, in future, by severe penalties. The triumph of the friends of freedom was graced by the confession of MR. CALHOUN, at the same session, that the efforts of the Abolitionists were of a moral and peaceful nature, and not, in his judgment, designed to provoke violence and insurrection.*

As the tide of reform could not be arrested either by mobs or proscriptive legislation, the final expedient of despotism was to crush the right of petition, and close the door of Congress to the great discussion. The right of Congress to abolish slavery in the Federal District and Territories, and to prohibit the domestic slave-trade, was extensively held; and the Abolitionists had persistently petitioned both houses to

* Goodell, pp. 421, 422.

exercise their constitutional powers over these evils. In order to exclude these dangerous influences, the slave power in Congress procured the adoption of a series of measures, known as the "gag-laws," which continued binding from May, 1836, to December, 1845. The efforts of JOHN QUINCY ADAMS to restore the right of petition deserve special mention. They constitute the crowning glory of his public life, as their success signalized the final triumph of the principle of freedom, in the North, over the ignoble coalition formed to overthrow it.

X.

NEW POLITICAL ORGANIZATIONS.—THE REPUBLICAN PARTY.

Decisive issue having been thus taken with the Southern despotism, and the right to discuss the evils of slavery being thus triumphantly sustained, the organization of new political parties — in order to give expression at the polls to the new convictions springing up at the North — became an inevitable consequence. The Liberty party, the Free-Soil party, and the Republican party, represent the successive stages of political action that were developed in the progress of the great reform inaugurated by the Abolitionists.

Meantime the original anti-slavery organizations became divided, and extensively modified, under the action of an irresistible individualism in some of the leaders, and as new exigencies appeared to call for new measures. Those iron bodies which had so gallantly sustained the hostility of a degenerate nation became prolific in issues, in controversies, and in dissent; and were in some danger of surrendering to faction part of the honors they had extorted from tyranny.

In 1844, the American Anti-Slavery Society, under the intrepid guidance of MR. GARRISON and the caustic eloquence of WENDELL PHILLIPS, proclaimed the new watchword, "NO UNION WITH SLAVE-HOLDERS," and denounced the Federal Constitution as "a covenant with death and an agreement with hell." This new position cost the Society many of its members; and it is believed that a large majority of the Abolitionists still hold that the Constitution is essentially a covenant with freedom, and that it is perverted when so construed as to sanction any interest of despotism.

The sentiment which animated the first reformers, in their vigorous assault upon the slave power, became *deteriorated* as it spread among the multitudes of the North, till the feeling which had originally demanded the immediate abolition of slavery became content with prohibiting its extension. The anti-slavery sentiment, thus deteriorated, obtained a rapid ascendency over the free States. The entire vote of the Liberty party at the Presidential election of 1840 amounted to something less than 7,000. Four years later, the candidates of that party received upwards of 60,000 votes; although it was well understood, that on neither occasion did the nominees of the party receive the votes of more than a fraction of the nominal Abolitionists in the United States, — some hundreds of them avoiding the polls from conscientious scruples, and the majority, influenced by old political ties, giving their support to the Whig and Democratic candidates.

When, in 1848, the Buffalo Platform appeared, *minus* the Abolition plank, it became at once evident that it would conciliate an augmented anti-slavery vote. The vote of the Free-Soil party that year, and of the Republican party in 1856, revealed an auspicious growth of the diluted anti-slavery sentiment which the North was prepared to express; and in 1860 two millions of Electors, in the face of the frantic threat of Disunion, solemnly decided that slavery should never again be extended under the flag of the nation.

XI.

CONSIDERATIONS.

Whether the Republican Party, in securing this decisive ascendency over the Northern mind, was *obliged* to take a lower moral position than the radical Abolitionists, — refusing to regard slavery as a crime *per se*, like murder or theft, but treating it as a social and political error, a source of practical evils deplorable and self-destructive, and a clear violation of those enlightened principles embodied in our form of government, — we do not propose to inquire. Whether, instead of advocating immediate and unconditional emancipation, it was wise in conceding to the South the common interpretation of the Constitution, under which slavery in the States is believed to be protected, we shall not here discuss. And whether, in going no further than to insist that the Federal Government should be divorced from the slave-holding propaganda, that slavery should be restricted to its present limits, and that its actual extinction should be left to the process of time, under the subduing force of moral and economical agencies, the party made the strongest possible appeal to the judgment and conscience of the American people, is not the question for present examination.

In consenting to such a disposal of the subject, there is no doubt that a large proportion of that party made some compromise between their principles and the exigency of the time. It seemed the only ground on which the North could cordially unite, and the Republic be delivered from the pro-slavery dynasty. It was not what the more earnest and enlightened members of the party *wanted*, we believe, but it seemed to comprise all that could be *secured* by undoubted constitutional means.

Hence the party were content to accept it as the best result attainable, under all the circumstances,—trusting that a new administration conscientiously devoted to the welfare of the whole nation, and of necessity hostile to the sectional purposes of slavery, might introduce a Federal policy, which, uniting with all the better tendencies of the Republic, should peacefully abolish the great crime of the land.

Still, it was placing the subject, at best, where the fathers had left it; and IGNORING THE DREADFUL LESSON WHICH THEIR TOLERATION OF SLAVERY HAD TAUGHT, and which the nation, one would have supposed, should have laid to heart. It was RELYING UPON THE SAME FALLACIOUS GUARANTIES WHICH HAD DECEIVED THE FOUNDERS OF THE GOVERNMENT, AND ALLOWING SLAVERY ANOTHER CHANCE TO SUBJUGATE THE REPUBLIC. The architects of the Union had erected a barrier to the progress of slavery, which the exulting despotism had triumphantly scaled, and the highest political wisdom of the country, enlightened by the experience of eighty years, could devise no better security for freedom than to rebuild the very WALL which slavery, with not one tenth of its present vigor, had been able to batter down.

The question will rise in the thoughtful mind, whether — had the South been content to abide the decision of the American people in 1860 — the instincts of slavery, so long active in the government, might not have been too potent for the integrity of the new administration, — aided by the advantage it still retained in both houses of Congress, — and whether the fair hopes built upon MR. LINCOLN'S elevation to the Presidency, might not have withered in the distant result.

Possibly our fond assurance might have proved our snare. Possibly Providence was more merciful to the land than it seemed, in releasing the wild-fire of rebellion. Possibly the Divine Omniscience perceived that the only road to national emancipation and permanent security led through the searching ordeal of civil war.

PART IV.

THE REBELLION OF THE BARONS.

" The well-known opinions of the Fathers were all discarded, and it was recklessly avowed that slavery is a divine institution, — the highest type of civilization, — a blessing to master and slave alike, — and the very keystone of our national arch. A generation has grown up with this teaching, so that it is now ready to say, with Satan,

' Evil, be thou my good; by thee at least
Divided empire with Heaven's King I hold;
As man erelong and this new world shall know.' "

HON. CHARLES SUMNER.

" To humor the present disposition and temporize, is a certain, absolutely certain confirmation of the evil. No nation ever did, or ever can, recover from slavery by such methods." — CHARLES JAMES FOX, 1804.

" Slavery is a system made up of every crime that treachery, cruelty, and murder can invent." — REV. ROWLAND HILL.

" Slavery is a complicated system of iniquity." — GRANVILLE SHARP.

"Whatever is morally wrong cannot be politically right." — JEFFERSON.

"By the law of God, unchangeable and eternal, while men despise fraud, and loathe rapine, and abhor bloodshed, they shall reject with indignation the wild and guilty fantasy, that man can hold property in man." — LORD BROUGHAM, 1830.

"While slavery lasts, it must continue, in addition to the actual amount of suffering and wrong which it entails on the enslaved, to operate with terrible reaction on the dominant class, to blunt the moral sense, to sap domestic virtue, to degrade independent industry, to check the onward march of enterprise, to sow the seeds of suspicion, alarm, and vengeance, in both internal and external intercourse, to distract the national counsels, to threaten the permanence of the Union, and to leave a brand, a byword, and a jest upon the name of Freedom." — EARL OF CARLISLE, 1851.

I.

THE PLOT OF AARON BURR.

THE rebellion, whose complete maturity and prolific resources appalled the nation during the revelations of the past winter (1860 – 61) is now known to be the product of assiduous intrigues, extending through not less than thirty years. And this great and criminal enterprise of our day really connects itself — not unnaturally — with certain alarming transactions that startled the quietude of the country as far back as 1807.

The arrest of COLONEL AARON BURR, that year, on charge of high treason, sent a thrill of amazement through the entire country. The eminent position of the accused, the turpitude of the alleged crime, and the probable magnitude to which the conspiracy had attained, all tended to inspire a deep and far-reaching sensation. Nor were the circumstances attending the trial and acquittal of BURR less surprising than the crime which had been charged upon him. In the light of the full-grown conspiracy of the present day, the memorable plot of 1807 may receive a more complete elucidation.

A shining character in every position he had

occupied, — a skilful military man, an adroit politician, an accomplished actor in society, — COLONEL BURR had been separated from the Presidency by only a single vote; and had occupied, under MR. JEFFERSON, the second official dignity in the executive department of the Republic. Unable to cope with the popularity of JEFFERSON, BURR became alienated from the Democratic party. Aware of his changed feelings, a portion of the Federal party in the State of New York began to esteem him an available candidate for the office of Governor. But GENERAL HAMILTON, a leading Federalist, opposed thc nomination of BURR, and denounced him as a man "dangerous to the country." For having used this language, HAMILTON was shot dead in a duel, having accepted a challenge from COLONEL BURR. Whether the strong expression HAMILTON had employed in allusion to his antagonist was only the utterance of partisan or personal antipathy, or whether it indicated an actual knowledge, or strong suspicion, of his treasonable purposes, — as many were afterwards inclined to believe, — cannot now be ascertained. It appears certain, however, from what was proved at the trial, and from guarded disclosures subsequently made, that BURR about this time was in the habit of making secret overtures to prominent men, and revealing the vague outlines of a gigantic scheme of disunion and conquest, to culminate in a magnificent Southern Empire. It is not known how far he obtained assurances of co-operation, for most of the evidence — as we shall presently see — was suppressed, and those who declined to participate in his plans seem to have been restrained from divulging them.

The plot was exposed by the following means: —

General William Eaton, of Massachusetts, had been American Consul at Tunis during our war with the Barbary States. In an expedition against Tripoli, which he had been authorized by his government to lead, he had won a brilliant reputation for military genius and personal bravery, and had honorably terminated our naval war in the Mediterranean. General Eaton had returned to America, a lauded hero, worthy of the honors he wore. But, being a New Englander and a Federalist, he had received but a cool reception at the seat of government. Certain sentiments hostile to slavery, which he had communicated in letters to his wife, and which had found their way into the newspapers, are said to have created a prejudice against him at the South, and to have influenced the government in its churlish recognition of his services. His accounts were disputed and disallowed, his integrity aspersed, and the basest attempts were made to dishonor him in the estimation of his country. Triumphantly vindicated from all the charges, but reduced by the government he had served to bankruptcy, he had retired in disgust from the public service.

In this mood he was approached by Colonel

BURR, who — judging him by his own standard of honor, and counting on his willingness to resent his injuries — proceeded to unfold his scheme. "He told EATON that he had already organized a secret expedition against the Spanish provinces of Mexico, in which he asked him to join; and EATON, under the impression, as he said, that the expedition was secretly countenanced by government — to which the state of Spanish relations and the Miranda expedition, then on foot, might well give color — gave him encouragement that he would. BURR then proceeded to further confidences, such as excited suspicions in EATON'S mind as to the real character of his intended enterprise. . . . . . Wishing, according to his own account, to draw BURR out, EATON encouraged him to go on, till finally he developed a project for revolutionizing the Western country, separating it from the Union, and establishing a monarchy, of which he was to be sovereign; New Orleans to be his capital; and his dominion to be further extended by a force organized on the Mississippi, so as to include a part or the whole of Mexico."

He represented that GENERAL WILKINSON, the commander-in-chief of the army, and recently appointed Governor of the Louisiana Territory, had become a party to the enterprise. "There was no energy in the government to be dreaded," it having become already paralyzed by party divisions. "Many enterprising men, who aspired to something beyond the dull pursuits of civil life," were ready to unite in the undertaking. "The promise of an immediate distribution of land, with the mines of Mexico in prospect, would call multitudes to his standard. Warming up with the subject, he declared that, if he could only secure the Marine Corps — the only soldiers stationed at Washington — and gain over the naval commanders, TRUXTON, PREBLE, DECATUR, and others, he would turn Congress neck and heels out of doors, assassinate the President, seize on the treasury and navy, and declare himself the protector of an energetic government. To which EATON, according to his own statement, replied, that one single word, USURPER, would destroy him, and that, though he might succeed at Washington in the first instance, within six weeks after he would have his throat cut by the Yankee militia."*

GENERAL EATON lost no time in communicating BURR's designs to the government; but, not enjoying the favor of the Administration, his important disclosures appear to have made no considerable impression, until confirmed by a despatch from GENERAL WILKINSON. In due time, BURR, BLENNERHASSET, and other supposed accomplices, were arrested, and brought to trial under an indictment for high treason found by a Grand Jury for the District of Virginia. CHIEF JUSTICE MARSHALL presided, holding the court in conjunction with GRIFFIN, the District Judge.

BURR was charged first with high treason; and

* Hildreth's History of the United States, Vol. V. pp. 600, 601.

second with a high misdemeanor, in attempting the invasion of Mexico, a Spanish province. The testimony of EATON and WILKINSON, it was generally supposed, would convict him; but theirs comprised but a fractional part of the testimony in the hands of the prosecuting attorney. Attempts were made to destroy the credit of both these witnesses, but without success. The acquittal was secured, however, by what has the appearance of a stratagem, though perhaps no artifice was intended. "The indictment was so drawn up as to charge him *only* with treasonable acts or misdemeanors committed by him on Blennerhasset's Island," in the Ohio River, while the principal part of the *evidence* in the hands of the prosecution had respect to acts committed *elsewhere.* Owing to this form of the indictment, "almost all the important testimony was excluded by the court from coming before the jury." The evidence of BLENNERHASSET was likewise excluded. It is thought that the jury suspected the court of some design to shield the accused, judging by the following verdict, which was read by COLONEL CARRINGTON, their foreman: "We, of the jury, say that AARON BURR is not proved guilty *under this indictment*, by any evidence *submitted to us.* We therefore find him not guilty." To this verdict exceptions were taken, for the reason that it seemed to "censure the court for suppressing irrelevant testimony." But, since the jury "would not agree to alter it, the court decided that the verdict should remain as found, and that an entry should be made on the record of not guilty."*

The acquittal of BURR is not easily explained by any facts that have yet been brought to light. The interest created by the trial was greatly imbittered by partisan influences. Many of the Federalists, having taken BURR into favor, and not being disposed, perhaps, to censure any conspiracy that threatened ruin to the Jefferson government, became zealous champions of the accused. On the other hand, the Democratic party, feeling that the honor of the Administration required a thorough ventilation of the plot, exerted itself to procure his conviction.

The progress of the trial gave rise to many rumors, which the dispassionate historian will probably disregard, unless subsequent disclosures shall lend confirmation to some of them. "So extensive and so powerful was the conspiracy found to be, and so wide-spread appeared to be the sympathy of the South with the prisoners, that it was feared at one time during the trial that, whether the arraigned were condemned or acquitted, the enterprise would in some way be resumed. It was currently understood that prominent men at the South, who were as deeply implicated as COLONEL BURR, and who were in fact the originators of the

* Burr's Trial, Reported by David Robertson, Esq., Vol. II. pp. 446, 447.

plot, were not arrested because it was not deemed prudent to proceed further. Among other rumors, one was that Colonel Burr was about to turn state's evidence against some of them, to procure indemnity for himself."

II.

THE IMAGE OF A SOUTHERN EMPIRE.—NULLIFICATION.

WHETHER the South was extensively implicated in BURR'S conspiracy or not, it is certain that the image of a Southern Empire, which he was probably the first to evoke, never faded from the Southern imagination. It has remained from that day a sort of political and social ideal, which time was to fulfil, and the genius of the South realize, whenever the nation should decide that her peculiar interest was no longer to be paramount in the Union. From the earliest intrigues of the slaveholders for the dismemberment of Mexico to the late efforts of WALKER to pioneer slavery into Central America, the rapacious craft of the oligarchy has been aiming at the organization of a vast polity on the model of AARON BURR'S exploded enterprise.

In every epoch of sectional excitement, in every period of discontent with the Federal Government, this idea of separation from the Republic, and the establishment of an independent confederacy, has been revived and propagated. In 1818, in the great struggle on the Missouri question, the dissolution of the Union was threatened, and probably meditated. JEFFERSON and others evidently considered the disastrous event as then impending.

In 1825, when the State of Georgia was brought in collision with the Federal Government on the question of making war upon the Indian tribes, the Southern Confederacy was foreshadowed in language pregnant with insurrection. "The hour is come, or is rapidly approaching, when the States from Virginia to Georgia, from Missouri to Louisiana, must CONFEDERATE, and as one man say to the Union: 'We will no longer submit our constitutional rights to bad men in Congress or on judicial benches,'" (the Supreme Court not having then espoused the slave-holding interest). "'The powers necessary to the protection of the confederated States from enemies without and within, *and these alone*, were confided to the United Government.'"

Again, in 1830, when the South had failed to coërce the Federal Government into a reduction or abolition of the tariff, South Carolina, under the direction of MR. CALHOUN, then Vice-President, ran up the seditious banner of Nullification, "forbade all levy of imposts under the regulations of the tariff, and refused to recognize the appeal which might be made to the Federal courts, declaring that South Carolina 'acknowledges no tribunal upon earth above her authority.'" About the time of the passage of this decree, MR. CALHOUN gave expression to that fruitful sentence which has developed, in the genial atmosphere of the South, into the practical doctrine of Secession:

"The Constitution is a compact to which the States were parties in their SOVEREIGN CAPACITY; now, whenever a compact is entered into by parties which acknowledge *no tribunal above their authority* to decide in the last resort, each of them has a right to judge for itself in relation to the nature, extent, and obligations of the instrument."

The practical comment of the Palmetto State upon these doctrines of her Legislature and her favorite chief, was to fill her towns with the clamor of military preparation, and fling out her seditious ensigns. Blue cockades and palmetto buttons were displayed. A red flag was unfurled, with a lone black star in the centre. The Federal banner was exhibited with the stars downward. Medals were struck, bearing the inscription, "JOHN C. CALHOUN, *First President of the Southern Confederacy!*"

To avert the threatened insurrection, GENERAL JACKSON strengthened the military posts in the rebellious State, and stationed a naval force off Charleston. In talking over the aspect of affairs, he said to GENERAL DALE: "If this thing goes on, our country will be like a bag of meal with both ends open. Pick it up in the middle or endwise, and it will run out. I must tie the bag, and save the country." When questioned, on his death-bed, as to what he would have done with CALHOUN and the Nullifiers in case they had persisted, he promptly answered: "Hung them, sir, as high as Haman. They should have been a terror to traitors to all time, and posterity would have pronounced it the best act of my life."

Posterity must indeed regret, that, instead of the vigorous measures which the President seemed inclined to adopt, a spirit of timidity and compromise was exhibited toward the insurgents. The pusillanimous attitude of the Federal Government, at that time quailing before a rebellious State, bore appropriate fruit, thirty years later, in the treasonable act of Secession, and in the piratical seizure of the property of the nation.

III.

PECULIAR SOCIAL SYSTEM OF THE SOUTH. — THE REBELLION THE LOGICAL RESULT.

THESE disunion tendencies have been awakened and stimulated, as no man can reasonably doubt, by that despotic principle which has always been supreme at the South, and of which slavery is the popular manifestation. That principle had already become so potent, in the days of the Revolution, that South Carolina had been induced only by laborious efforts to adopt the Declaration of Independence, and had not been restrained, in the struggle that ensued, from tendering her submission to the British crown.* The same principle had been so far dominant in the Southern mind, in the days of the Constitutional Convention, that MR. RUTLEDGE, of South Carolina, had said, while opposing a tax on the importation of slaves: "The true question at present is, whether Southern States shall or shall not be parties to the Union." And MR. PINCKNEY had followed with the odious sentiment, that South Carolina would never receive the Constitution if it prohibited the slave-trade.†

* Hon. Charles Sumner's Address at Cooper Institute, Nov. 27, 1861. Compare Hildreth's History, Vol. III. p. 280.

† Elliott's Debates, Vol. V. p. 457.

As far back as March, 1776, JOHN ADAMS had declared, — writing to GENERAL GATES, — "All our misfortunes arise from a single source, the *resistance of the Southern Colonies to republican government*." And he adds, that "popular principles and axioms are abhorrent to the inclinations of the BARONS OF THE SOUTH." *

Facts have come to light during only the past year which conclusively show that the idea of dismembering the Union had been for a long time the settled purpose of the Southern leaders, and that, too, without respect to the conduct of the North, — the alleged grievances being only pretexts to cover this all-pervading policy of rebellion, and gloss the odious atrocity of treason.

In a confidential letter written by Jackson, in 1833, and only recently made public, he says, in allusion to the Nullification movement: "The Tariff was only the *pretext*, and DISUNION and a SOUTHERN CONFEDERACY the *real object*. THE NEXT PRETEXT WILL BE THE NEGRO OR SLAVERY QUESTION."

The statement of JACKSON is most emphatically confirmed by the confessions made in the Rebel Convention of South Carolina. MR. PACKER reminds his fellow-traitors, that "Secession is no spasmodic effort that has come suddenly upon us. It has been gradually culminating for a long series of years." MR. INGLIS said: "Most of us have had this subject under consideration for the last

* John Adams's Works, Vol. I. p. 207.

twenty years." MR. KEITT ardently declared: "I have been engaged in this movement ever since I entered political life." MR. RHETT confessed: "It is nothing produced by MR. LINCOLN'S election, or the non-execution of the Fugitive Slave Law. It is a matter which has been gathering head for thirty years."

The real ground of Southern discontent, the true spring of the movement for dissolution, has been candidly admitted by DR. SMYTHE, of Charleston: "It is not the election of a Republican President, nor the non-execution of the Fugitive Slave Law. The real difficulty lies far back of these things. It consists in the atheistic, Red Republican doctrine of the Declaration of Independence; and until this is trampled under foot, there can be no peace."* Here we have the *ultimatum* of despotism; the entire abrogation of liberty as the condition of peace!

It may be readily seen how the growth of this conspiracy resulted inevitably from the social system of the South. As the devotion of those communities to slavery became confirmed by commercial cupidity and the interests of political ambition, — as a degenerate sentiment began to rally in defence of slavery, as a lawful and permanent institution, — as the moral sense became coerced into an acceptance of the system, and the popular passions enlisted in its perpetuity, — it re-

* Quoted from memory.

sulted of necessity that the entire South should assume an attitude of vigilance, of suspicion, and of hostility toward whatever influences appeared to endanger her precarious possessions. The incompatibility of the slave system with the most obvious principles of a republican government could hardly fail to have been detected, at an early day, by the wakeful guardians of the slave power. The very form, the paramount ideas, of the Federal Government, — to say nothing of the well-known opinions of most of its framers, — were seen to be hostile to slavery. It was felt from the first, that, under such a government, slavery could hope only for a precarious toleration; and that, if the people were ever to demand a general enforcement of its principles, the incongruous system must be swept from the land. It subsisted, thus far, by the sufferance of the nation, rather than by any legitimate authority that could be justly claimed for its support. All legitimate authority was against it, because the common law, the national law, nature, and conscience were against it. It was a licentious robber, bolted within one of the apartments of the house, defying the magistrate, it is true, but fearfully exposed to the slumbering justice which he was authorized to execute. Who could tell when that righteous Christian sentiment which abhors slavery as the foulest of wrongs, omnipotent already in other countries, might attain so great an ascendency in this, as to demand the abolition of the gigantic iniquity? What permanent safety could be found for the slave system, except by sundering the States that nourished it from the dangerous contagion of a free nation, and casting off the authority of the Constitution, whose avowed object it is to establish justice and secure the blessings of liberty?

Moreover, though the American people had hitherto been induced to favor slavery, by a series of astonishing concessions to its illegal demands, the irrepressible tendency of free society had brought the slave system into condemnation. Defer to slavery as tamely as men would, — apologize, intrigue, and vote for it as they might, — they could not change those laws of the Almighty which bring blessings upon free labor, and all the glories of civilization to free States, while they infuse curses into the profits of tyranny, and sink the empire that espouses it into barbarism. It had become plain that no craft could tamper with the equity of Providence, however shamefully depraved might become the government. That dread equity had drawn a black judicial line between the free and slave States, displaying on one side thrift, refinement, intelligence, order, and the tender charities that spring from Christian culture, and disclosing on the other, indigence, brutality, ignorance, incipient anarchy, and heathen cruelty.

A contrast so vivid, in which God had apparently impressed his approval of freedom and his detestation of tyranny, was not to be withstood without imminent peril of the eventful judgment of man's awakened conscience and reason. The preservation of slavery required that it should be rescued from the condemnation of such a contrast; shielded from the competition of free labor; furnished with clear constitutional sanctions, and invested with the spoils of Mexico and Cuba, with whatever additional lands might be cloven out of the Western Hemisphere to feed its rapacious lust.

Hence all the fierce impulses of the Southern blood leaped in the line of Disunion. A besotted devotion to the slave system, and a fanatical hatred of the liberal principles embodied in the Republic, became paramount passions. Secret machinations to undermine the government, and a growing jealousy and antipathy toward the free States, became characteristic of the Southern politicians and people. Adopting the fervid rhetoric of one of their orators, we may say, that "the lone star of their empire attracted their political needle to the tropics," there to develop a social system grounded on the everlasting subjugation of the African.

To that infatuated people — lured by the baleful phantom their cruelty and pride have evoked — it has seemed a small thing to become alienated from the principles and hopes of the Republic; to conspire for thirty years against the life of the nation that honored them with its confidence, and to maintain whose authority they had registered their oaths in heaven ; to stand before the bar of mankind as the architects of a new nationality, based upon the worst form of oppression the world ever saw, and to become transfixed by the judgment of posterity as the most odious enemies of their race. Such is the fearful madness with which God humiliates the haughtiness of the wicked, while justice is arming its ministers to cut them off from the land.

IV.

THE RIPENING OF THE TREASON.

Meantime, so long as the Federal Government could be kept subservient to the extension of slavery, there was no motive for revolting against it. Inasmuch as that government was mainly supported by revenue drawn from the free States, and in consideration of its ductile fidelity to the slave policy, it was for the interest of the South still to acknowledge its authority. So long as the Federal Union could be made the instrument of slavery with very little comparative expense to the South, it was almost as convenient as a Southern Confederacy, and infinitely more economical.

So long as the master of the house evinced no symptoms of "a change of heart" in favor of liberty, there was no other reason for blowing up the edifice than a vindictive desire to injure some of the servants. Where, in all the slave-holding dominion, among all the hypothetical representatives of the despotic policy, could have been found two men more zealous for the interests of slavery than Presidents Pierce and Buchanan? Surely, the South might afford to possess its soul in patience; surely, it could safely venture to postpone the perilous experiment of rebellion. It has been said by persons apparently familiar with the Plutonian economy, that the Devil himself rests content when the ablest of his human parasites are actively furthering his cause.

But the free States were rousing. Burning words were being spoken, and deaf ears were being unstopped. Vital ideas were spreading from heart to heart, and the ghastly sepulchre of Democracy was giving up its dead. There were rising portents gathering in the Northern sky, that troubled the astrologers of the South. The emergency called for extreme measures. To break the Missouri contract, and pour slavery into the Northwest; to plant the death-bearing vine on the slopes of the Pacific; to nationalize kidnapping by turning the Federal law into a slave code; and to legalize the claim of property in man, in all the States and Territories, became the characteristic policy of the South. Failing in these measures, the tocsin of rebellion was to sound, and the black bird of treason batten on the dismembered nation.

In the struggle that ensued, the malignant nature of slavery was appallingly disclosed in its final efforts to maintain its ascendency. On the floor of Congress, in California, in Kansas, and in the courts of the slave-hunter, — under the exasperating conviction that the sceptre was departing from its control, — it perpetrated atrocities that amazed mankind. Nor were the most illustrious of our Senators safe from the bludgeon discipline which that despotism would fain have instituted in the halls of the Capitol.

The election of 1856, though it resulted in a new lease of power to the slave oligarchy, gave sure indications that a new dynasty was at hand. Such was the temper of the free States, and so vigorous and resolute had the spirit of liberty become, that it was morally certain a new policy must be initiated at no distant day. The time had come for the South to translate her treasonable theories into practical rebellion. The time had come to destroy the government which was about to be rescued from prostitution. The time had come to realize the long-cherished dream of a Southern Confederacy, to be built out of the wreck, and enriched by the plunder, of the Federal Union.

V.

FINAL ORGANIZATION OF THE PLOT IN MR. BUCHANAN'S CABINET.

NEVER had a gigantic conspiracy such liberal opportunity. Never had traitors such tremendous immunities. The government that was to be disorganized, the Republic that was to be dismembered, were wholly in the power of the Southern rebels and their Northern abettors.

The Cabinet of MR. BUCHANAN was honeycombed by this perfidious conspiracy. The Secretary of the Treasury was a slave-holder from Georgia; the Secretary of the Interior was a slave-holder from Mississippi; and the Secretary of War was a slave-holder from Virginia; — these men were all indefatigable in the work of treason. The Secretary of the Navy was a Northern man; but he seems not to have hesitated on that account to lend his active services to the plot. Among the four traitor Secretaries, MR. FLOYD, of Virginia, claims the pre-eminence in crime, — the revelations of his Department having proved him an adept in all grades of villany, extending from grand larceny to high treason. But what shall be the verdict of posterity on the conduct of the venerable President, who, during those years of maturing rebellion, was in the closest official intimacy with the conspirators? Was he so far demented as not to be aware of the nature of the enterprise that occupied the chief care of his Cabinet; or was he so irretrievably committed to the oligarchy that had elevated him, as to deliberately pledge his high prerogative to the ruin of the nation he had sworn to serve?

As MR. LINCOLN'S election became more and more probable, the conspiracy rapidly matured under the direction of the recreant functionaries who were depraving the highest Federal powers to its service. "Never before in any country was there a similar crime which embraced so many persons in the highest places of power, or which took within its grasp so large a theatre of human action."

By a series of secret measures concerted and directed by the Cabinet, almost every available resource was withdrawn from the government, in anticipation of its passing under a new administration. In the first place, "the army of the United States was so far dispersed and exiled that the commander-in-chief found it difficult, during the recent anxious winter, to bring together a thousand troops for the defence of the national capital, menaced by the conspirators." A similar disposition was made of the navy, so "that on the 4th of March, when the new Administration came into power, there were no ships to enforce the laws, collect the revenues, or protect the national property in the rebel ports." Out of seventy-two war-vessels that comprised the American navy, the *judicious* Secretary of that Department had left at home, for the emergency of the rebellion, the steamer *Brooklyn*, with twenty-five guns, and the store-ship *Relief*, armed with two guns. In the next place, "the forts on the extensive Southern coast were so far abandoned by the public force that the larger part — counting upwards of twelve hundred cannons, and built at a cost of upwards of six millions of dollars — became at once an easy prey to the rebels."

In the progress of these astounding proceedings, "national arms were transferred from Northern to Southern arsenals, so as to disarm the free States, and equip the slave States. This was done on a large scale. Upwards of one hundred and fifteen thousand arms of the latest and most improved pattern were transferred from the Springfield and Watervliet arsenals to different arsenals in the slave States, where they have been seized by the rebels. And a quarter of a million percussion muskets were sold to various slave States, at two dollars and a half a musket, when they were worth, it is said, on an average, twelve dollars. Large quantities of cannon, mortars, powder, ball, and shell received the same direction." Finally, "the national Treasury, which so recently had been prosperous beyond example, was disorganized and plundered to the verge of bankruptcy. Upwards of six millions are supposed to have been stolen, and much of this treasure doubtless went to help the work of rebellion." *

Meantime, in the election of 1860, two millions of American freemen recorded their verdict against any further toleration of the slave despotism. The better part of the nation rejoiced in the prospect of a new political dispensation. Little did they suspect that their government was already betrayed to that despotism from whose craft they fondly trusted they had rescued it! Little were they aware that Cabinet Ministers and Senators — in contempt of their solemn oaths and of every dictate of honor — had already laid the mine of treason under a dozen States, and were chuckling over the prospect of seeing the Union blown into fragments, as the original seceders in Pandemonium hailed with sardonic rapture the curse that was to fall upon Eden. By no means could our people conceive what horrible paradoxes were being exemplified in those last days of the pro-slavery dynasty, when the very highest organs of the Republic were ministering death to liberty; when the vaunting representatives of chivalry gloried in betraying their most sacred trusts; when the men who sat at the council board of the Chief Magistrate — esteeming loyalty a farce, and abasing truth before craft — were intriguing to supersede his legally-chosen successor, and to enthrone a military despotism in the Capitol.

* Address of Hon. Charles Sumner at Cooper Institute.

VI.

THE DRAMA OF INSURRECTION.

THE drama of insurrection — appropriately opened by South Carolina — rapidly extended to the other Gulf States. In all those States where slavery was omnipotent, the rebellion started to its feet, "like a strong man armed." It mattered not that those States had been purchased by Federal treasure, defended by Federal armies, and fostered by Federal patronage. It mattered not, that, in their weakness, in their poverty and semi-barbarism, the beneficent arms of the Republic had been cast around them, associating them in the honors and prospects of an illustrious nationality. It mattered not that, where a Texan refugee, a Mississippian repudiator, or a hanger of schoolmasters from Arkansas, would have been held abroad no better than a freebooter from the Spanish Main, the indorsement of the great Republic and the protection of the American flag had covered him with the immunities of citizenship, and passed him current round the globe.

With an impudence every way characteristic of slavery, they asserted the right to abandon, at their arbitrary pleasure, the Union to which they were so deeply indebted, to appropriate its property to their own uses, and to throw its great commercial artery, the Mississippi River, under a foreign jurisdiction.

In the startling developments of the insurrection, an incredible turpitude of duplicity and atrocity was unmasked. The crimes that had matured in secret came to be trumpeted from the house-tops. Men whom the favor of the Republic had enriched, found the Republic too poor to command their reverence. Men bred to the profession of arms at the nation's cost, turned their tactics against the nation's life. Men who had fatted on the patronage of the government throughout the long, luxurious day of peace, no sooner saw the government in danger, than they handed back their commissions, and stepped over to the rebel camp!

In that most critical hour — when treason seemed to have undermined every department of the government — only two eminent officials remained faithful to the imperilled Republic. The Commander-in-Chief, General Scott, who exerted all his energies to protect the capital; and the Secretary of State, General Cass, who is said to have persuaded the President to maintain the Federal flag at Fort Sumter, merit the unspeakable praise of having saved the nation, under the merciful providence of God, from falling irretrievably into the hands of the conspirators.

VII.

THE AGONY OF COMPROMISE.

While the insurrection was making such formidable progress at the South, the apathy that pervaded the North was not less remarkable.

During the earliest months of the Rebellion, our people were mildly debating whether the traitors were really in earnest, or whether they were not playing their favorite game of bluster, for the purpose of extorting new concessions; whether they would not presently repent and return, like the Prodigal; and whether it was good policy to coerce them into submission to the laws. Such blindness to the real issue that had risen — such insensibility to the actual danger that beset the national existence — was never witnessed before.

By the time Congress was ready to assemble, the insurrection was under full head, its defiant ground boldly taken, and its purposes audaciously declared. But even yet it was to be fostered and justified by the depraved Executive, and on no account resisted or exposed. In the Message of the President, as if to crown with becoming infamy a public career devoted to the slave power, — instead of recognizing the Rebellion in its truly atrocious character, and calling upon Congress to aid him in subduing it as they valued the nation's existence,—he proceeded to express open sympathy with the insurgents; to charge upon the North the responsibility of their acts; and to recommend on the part of the free States wholesale concessions to that aggressive oligarchy already standing armed at the Capitol gate for the murder of Liberty.

The ensuing proceedings, under the auspices of the government, that thus caressed its foes and maligned its friends, were equally inconsistent with the crisis, and equally disloyal to the demands of the hour. For example, what greater farce could have been played, to delude a nation hanging on the brink of ruin, than the Peace Conference, as it was impertinently named,—a meeting convened on the motion of the Virginia rebels, with JOHN TYLER in the chair,—a meeting which the North was so far deluded as to recognize, and to which she sent some of her most honored citizens? "The sessions were with closed doors, but it is now known that throughout the proceedings, lasting for weeks, nothing was discussed but slavery. And the propositions finally adopted by the Convention were confined to slavery. Forbearing all details, it will be enough to say that they undertook to give to slavery positive protection in the Constitution, with new sanction and immunity, making it—notwithstanding the determination of our fathers—national instead of sectional; and even more than this, making it one of the essential and permanent parts of our Republican system. . . . . . There was another string of propositions much discussed during the last winter, which bore the name of the venerable Senator from whom they came, MR. CRITTENDEN, of Kentucky. These also related to slavery, and nothing else. They were more obnoxious even than those emanating from the Peace Conference." The aim of these propositions was "to foist into the Constitution the idea of property in man; to protect slavery in all present territory south of thirty-six degrees thirty minutes, and to carry it into all territory hereafter acquired south of that line; to give new constitutional securities to slavery in the national capital, and in other places within the exclusive Federal jurisdiction"; and to insure the safe *transit* of slaves through the free States, thus contaminating every foot of our soil with the odious sanctions of tyranny.* Will the world believe that we were any longer worthy of liberty, when it is known that there were men at the North so lost to national dignity as to petition the Federal Congress to make that enormous surrender to the arch rebel and armed enemy of the Republic!

There was still another peace offering tendered to the defiant rebels; for the tendency to compromise with slavery had become chronic; and, with what EDWARD EVERETT happily terms "*a melan-*

* Hon. Charles Sumner.

choly assiduity," that craven Congress toiled to appease the slave-masters. We allude to MR. CORWIN's proposal, which became a legislative act, "that the Constitution shall not be so amended as to give Congress the power to abolish or interfere with slavery in the States."

Thus did the Union humiliate itself before its enemies, after their character and purposes had become fully disclosed! Thus did the Federal Government, so long subservient to slavery, betrayed, threatened, and despised, still lick the wicked hand that was clenched to annihilate it!

Without even affecting to hide the contempt they felt for the base overtures which had been made, "the Barons of the South" assembled at Montgomery, to organize their new government. Seven States were represented. The action of the Convention was rapid and decisive. After adopting the Federal Constitution, with a few characteristic modifications, — the rule being *to appropriate everything belonging to their late government that was available*, — it proceeded to organize "the nucleus of an army and navy," chose a President and Vice-President, demanded a loan of fifteen million dollars, levied an export duty on cotton, declared the Mississippi free, proposed a new tariff and navigation laws, and claimed a place in the family of nations as "the Confederate States of America."

VIII.

THE RIVAL ADMINISTRATIONS INAUGURATED IN THE DISMEMBERED REPUBLIC.

In his inaugural address, Jefferson Davis discreetly avoids unfolding the causes of the Secession movement, but says, explicitly, that "the judgment and will of the people are, that connection with the Northern States is neither practicable nor desirable"; and that, "if necessary, we must obtain by final arbitrament of the sword the position we have assumed."

We are indebted to the Vice-President, Mr. Stephens, for the frankest exposition of the cardinal principle of the new Confederacy. It is such as we were prepared to expect, from our acquaintance with the antecedents of the slave oligarchy. The principle is, that THE SUPERIOR RACE MUST CONTROL THE INFERIOR; in other words, that the strong must own the weak, and that might makes right. Mr. Stephens, after stating the ideas of the American Fathers, as embodied in the Declaration, — that "all men are created equal, being endowed by their Creator with inalienable rights to life, liberty, and the pursuit of happiness,"— stigmatizes them as furnishing "a sandy foundation" for society, and declares that the "new government is founded upon exactly the OPPOSITE IDEAS. Its foundations are laid, its corner-stone rests, upon the great truth that the negro is not equal to the white man; that slavery — subordination to the superior race — is his natural and normal condition."

But it is not the subordination of the negro alone that is contemplated by the rebel government. We have seen that HENRY CLAY anticipated that slavery would survive the negro race; and it is clear that the principle on which Southern society is based, and which is frankly avowed by MR. STEPHENS as the corner-stone of the new Confederacy, would promptly seize the weakest of the white race, in the absence of the black. In DE BOW'S Review, — which is acknowledged to be a fair organ of Southern opinion, — a writer calls for "a government based upon the principle of military subordination." He counsels the rulers of the South to procure such a modification of the State constitutions as to "remove the people further from power," and establish "an hereditary Senate and Executive."

These views, so consonant with the fundamental principle of the rebel government, have been acted upon in all the seceded States, — not only by the armed despotism which has impelled those States on the tide of treason, while expelling the loyal inhabitants from their borders, but in some legislative enactments tending to a monopoly of social privileges and rights.

In harmony with this cardinal law of the slave empire was the secret programme of the ensuing tragedy. The Capitol and the national archives were to be seized as early as March; the Plug-Uglies of Baltimore were to bring in MR. LINCOLN'S head upon a charger, while the daughter of Discord danced before the embodiment of Despotism; on the Fourth of July, the insurgents were to hold high carnival in Independence Hall; and the early autumn was to behold them hanging Abolitionists on Bunker Hill, — while the Christian nations of Europe, converted by the gospel of the London *Times*, were to render homage to King Cotton by recognizing the gigantic usurpation.

Fortunately for the country, there was an invisible agency — never absent from human affairs, but of which bad men make no account — that was silently thwarting the atrocious plot. JEFFERSON DAVIS and his satellites were born too late by five hundred years. The providence of God, which develops out of successive cycles an ever-augmenting sum of good for man, could not allow a type of government indigenous to the Middle Ages to become interpolated into the nobler text of the nineteenth century. We owe our rescue from the greatest crime ever meditated against civilization to the simple fact that the Divine order could not tolerate so violent an anachronism.

A change in the rebel programme may be traced to "the sudden act of MAJOR ANDERSON in removing from Fort Moultrie to Fort Sumter, and the sympathetic response of an aroused people." In that apparently trivial circumstance, the Rebellion received its first check. Washington was saved. The President elect, passing in disguise through seditious Baltimore, eluded the assassins, and reached the capital in safety. There the veteran SCOTT, beset by spies and traitors, was rallying the "forlorn hope" of the nation. There the retiring chief magistrate, bending under the contempt of his country, having prostituted every official prerogative to further the conspiracy, declared himself willing to ride with the new President to his inauguration. There were assembled excited citizens from all the loyal States, to witness the national ceremony which all felt was liable to end in a tragedy.

Never before had Washington presented so mournful and impressive a scene. "Around that tall, ungainly figure, which stood upon the steps of the Capitol above the multitude, more of fear, anxiety, and hope clustered than above any former President." He was himself penetrated by the solemnity of the moment. He had entered upon a course "the issues of which were hidden by the darkest clouds which had ever hung over his country. He saw the Union dismembered, full of dissension and full of fear, and realized that upon him more than upon any other man rested its future destinies. He saw arrayed against his rule a band of rebellious States; he saw that during his administration the strength of the government would be tested, — that Providence had called him to preside over the changes of a great historical epoch, and that the eyes of the civilized world were upon him. For the first time in American history, bayonets bristled and cannon frowned around the Federal Capitol. Familiar faces were seen no more; friends, whose presence had lent lustre to many preceding inaugurations, in distant States were ranged in the malignant attitude of foes; and every ear was strained to hear whether

> 'The long, stern swell
> Which bids the soldier close'

were coming up on the soft southern breezes. Seven States had seceded, others were hanging to the Union by a thread; — forts, arsenals, mints, sub-treasuries had been seized; Forts Sumter and Pickens were beleaguered; — insurgents were in possession of nearly every stronghold on the Atlantic, from North Carolina to the Texan frontier; and a hostile Congress and President, sitting at Montgomery, were providing the sinews of war, and threatening an appeal to the bloody arbitrament of the sword."

IX.

COMPROMISE ENDS, AND THE NEW ERA BEGINS.

In this unexampled exigency, the Inaugural Address of the new President was heard by the American people with an interest unfelt before. With all our partiality for the nation's choice, and with an unshaken confidence in the integrity of the man, we cannot admit that the Address was equal to the occasion, in any sense.

It failed to recognize the true character of the conspiracy; it undertook *to argue down an armed rebellion*, pervading nearly half the area of the country; it asserted that the laws must be executed in all the States, but disclaimed the intention of resorting to arms unless the rebels first drew the sword; and, worse than all, it affirmed the obligation of the statute for the rendition of fugitive slaves; thus holding out another fruitless concession to that disdainful oligarchy, which it was obvious nothing could reach but the terrors of the law they had violated and contemned.

It may be urged, however, in justification of the pacific tone of the Inaugural Address, that the conciliatory policy thus intimated was deemed necessary to retain the border States from drifting into the baleful current of Secession; and that the President consulted his official dignity by forbearing to menace the traitors so long as the demoralized government furnished him no resources to enforce his authority. The critical ground on which MR. LINCOLN confessedly stood, as well as the limitations of our common nature, will doubtless excuse him at the tribunal of history for the utterance of words so disproportionate to the emergency, and for an apparent reliance upon bland admonitions, which the turpitude of the Rebellion had rendered obviously impotent.

The pacificating policy ended with the assault upon Fort Sumter. The civil war, which sagacious men had long foreseen to be inevitable, was formally initiated when the national flag was struck from that fortress.

The two antagonistic systems, whose moral collision had formed the drama of our politics, had now closed in a physical conflict which could result only in the annihilation of one of them.

The Barons of the South had made their deliberate appeal to the sword, as the champions of a worse than feudal despotism; and time alone could declare whether Liberty would find effectual succor in the degenerate Republic.

PART V.

THE PROVIDENTIAL ALTERNATIVE.

"For Civil War, that it is an evil I dispute not. But that it is the greatest of evils, that I stoutly deny. It doth indeed appear to the misjudging to be a worse calamity than bad government, because its miseries are collected within a short space and time, and may easily, at one view, be taken in and perceived. . . . . . When the devil of Tyranny hath gone into the body politic, he departs not but with struggles, and foaming, and great convulsions. Shall he, therefore, vex it forever, lest, in going out, he for a moment tear and rend it?" — MILTON.

"It is impossible for a nation, even while struggling for itself, not to acquire something for all mankind." — MOTLEY.

"Horrid, atrocious, and impious Slavery covered with her sable mantle the land of Venezuela, and our atmosphere lowered with the dark, gloomy clouds of the tempest, threatening a fiery deluge. I implored the protection of the God of nature, and at His almighty word the storm was dispelled. The day-star of Liberty arose. Slavery broke her chains, and Venezuela was surrounded with new and grateful sons, who turned the instruments of her thrall and bondage into the arms of Freedom. Yes, those who were formerly slaves are now free; those who were formerly enemies of our country are now its defenders. I leave to your sovereign authority the reform or repeal of all my ordinances, statutes, and decrees. But I implore you to confirm the complete emancipation of the slaves, as I would beg my life or the salvation of the Republic." — GENERAL BOLIVAR *to the Congress of Venezuela.*

"AS GOD LIVES AND REIGNS, EITHER THIS NATION WILL ABOLISH SLAVERY, OR SLAVERY WILL ABOLISH IT!" — HON. GERRIT SMITH.

"Then Freedom sternly said: 'I shun
No strife nor pang beneath the sun,
When human rights are staked and won.

"'I knelt with Ziska's hunted flock,
I watched in Toussaint's cell of rock,
I walked with Sidney to the block.

"'The moor of Marston felt my tread,
Through Jersey snows the march I led,
My voice Magenta's charges sped.

"'But now, through weary day and night,
I watch a vague and aimless fight
For leave to strike one blow aright.

"'On either side my foe they won:
One guards through love his ghastly throne,
And one through fear to reverence grown.

"'Why wait we longer, mocked, betrayed
By open foes or those afraid
To speed thy coming through my aid?

"'Why watch to see who win or fall? —
I shake the dust against them all,
I leave them to their senseless brawl.'

"'Nay,' Peace implored: 'yet longer wait;
The doom is near, the stake is great;
God knoweth if it be too late.

"'Still wait and watch; the way prepare
Where I with folded wings of prayer
May follow, weaponless and bare.'

"'Too late!' the stern, sad voice replied,
'Too late!' its mournful echo sighed,
In low lament the answer died.

"A rustling as of wings in flight,
An upward gleam of lessening white,
So passed the vision, sound and sight.

"But round me, like a silver bell
Rung down the listening sky to tell
Of holy help, a sweet voice fell.

"'Still hope and trust,' it sang; 'the rod
Must fall, the wine-press must be trod,
But all is possible with God!'"

John G. Whittier.

I.

GLOOMY ASPECT OF THE STRUGGLE.

THE Rebellion that put off its disguise and assumed the defiant panoply of war in April last, extended over an area of 733,144 square miles. It possessed a coast line of 3,523 miles, and a shore line of 25,414 miles, with an interior boundary line of 7,031 miles in length.* From the immense region here indicated, it boasted that it could enlist and place in the field 600,000 men.

To oppose an insurrection covering such space of territory, and embracing an armed force among the largest ever marshalled in war, what resources did the nation possess? The Rebellion had, under the toleration and by the connivance of the late Administration, scattered the navy of the United States to the uttermost parts of the globe; demoralized and betrayed the army; stripped the loyal States of arms to equip those embarked in the insurrection; obtained possession of about every fortress, arsenal, sub-treasury, mint, within the lines of the conspiracy; completely plundered the United States Treasury, and sapped with trea-

* Report of the Secretary of War, December, 1861.

son all the pillars of the Republic. In short, while the Rebellion was affluent in every material resource, — resolute, sanguine, rapacious, vigilant, indefatigable, — the Union was literally despoiled, the new government defenceless, apparently vacillating, temporizing with its unmeasured fate, embarrassed in every function, and so completely girded by sedition and anarchy, that some of the earliest troops — hastening from a free State to its rescue — fell victims to rebel treachery in the streets of Baltimore.

Under these gloomy auspices, the great struggle commenced. On one side, the oligarchy of Slave Barons, armed and aggrandized with the stolen resources of the nation; on the other, the dismantled Republic, with no reliance but a plundered government and the patriotic loyalty of the legitimate heirs of freedom. To the outward view, never was a great conflict begun under so great a disparity of resources.

II.

THE REBELLION VULNERABLE THROUGH SLAVERY.

AND yet it was evident from the first, to all who apprehended the real *animus* of the contest, that the Rebellion presented one vulnerable point, where it was easy to strike it a mortal blow. Slavery was the notorious spring of the Rebellion. The motive power of the Rebellion was the heart-beat of slavery, aspiring to crush the continent in its snaky embrace. Let the Federal power, in the exercise of either its civil or military prerogative, launch one resolute, mortal shaft into the heart of slavery, and the Rebellion would sink lifeless in a day.

It was observed that the degree to which people were enamored of slavery described the exact extent of their devotion to the Rebellion. Thus South Carolina and Georgia, Alabama and Mississippi, Louisiana and Texas, are the States most ardently espoused to slavery; and these, accordingly, were the chief seats of the great conspiracy. In the States less interested in slavery — North Carolina, Tennessee, Virginia — the Rebellion found less encouragement, and prevailed only by a process of despotic intimidation and mobocratic violence. In those border States — Maryland, Kentucky, and Missouri — where the popular interest in slavery is comparatively lukewarm, all efforts to achieve disunion were defeated, although the slave element in those States, creating sympathies and animosities favorable to the Rebellion, has faithfully succored and abetted the cause to which it bears affinity.

It was observed, also, that the cardinal doctrine of the Rebellion — the alleged right of a State to nullify the Federal Constitution and sever its connection with the Union — was a logical outgrowth of that usurpation which slavery involves. The doctrine "belongs to that brood of assumptions and perversions of which slavery is the prolific parent. Wherever slavery prevails, this pretended right is recognized, and generally with an intensity proportioned to the prevalence of slavery, — as, for instance, in South Carolina and Mississippi more intensely than in Tennessee and Kentucky. It may be considered a fixed part of the slave-holding system. A pretended right to set aside the Constitution to the extent of breaking up the government, is the natural companion to the pretended right to set aside human nature to the extent of making merchandise of men." The doctrine of Secession is instinct with the lawlessness of slavery. The system that finds toleration in the crime of overthrowing the very *nature of man* could not be expected to hesitate in overturning a mere form of government. The greater crime which our nation had consented to ignore includes the less which has startled us from our apathy.

It was notorious that the extension and protection of slavery furnished the sole motive to the Rebellion. But for the perpetuity of slavery, there could never have been any incentive to secession, or any conflict of interest in the nation. Only let the terrors of our violated federal law fall upon slavery, the clearly convicted criminal, — only let it suffer the destruction which its crimes had justly provoked, — and all the hopes that inspired and nourished the Rebellion must likewise perish.

The slave system being annihilated, the project of a Southern Confederacy having slavery for its corner-stone would be forever dissipated. The one only impediment to Union would be removed, — the stone of offence, the element of discord, the arch-author of sedition, would be swept from the land, — leaving to the Northern and Southern sections of the Republic a common interest, a kindred ambition, and a united career of prosperity and glory.

These considerations were so obvious that they flashed through the minds of thoughtful men at the very opening of the drama, and revealed to them what appeared to be the imperative policy of the government. God had put the duty of our rulers before the people in so clear a light that it seemed no prejudice or casuistry would be able to hide it. He had so disposed events as to make the rescue of the nation dependent on the destruction of slavery ; while he had obviously connected the preservation of slavery with the annihilation of the Union. Surely now there could be no hesitation. The fate of the slave had become identified with the fate of the Republic. A decree of national justice had become the indispensable means of national redemption. The law of self-preservation had become the law of liberty.

III.

IMPRACTICABLE POLICY OF THE GOVERNMENT. — PROTECTING SLAVERY AT THE EXPENSE OF THE UNION. — DESTROYING THE NATION TO SAVE ITS CONSTITUTION.

WILL a future generation be able to credit the amazing fact, that — during the earlier months of the war — our Government apparently ignored all these considerations, sedulously affected to overlook the criminality of slavery as the chief agency and paramount interest of the Rebellion, and attempted a fallacious discrimination between the overt act of treason and the instigating cause and covert inspiration thereof? Yet such was the suicidal policy under which our first battalions, obeying the summons of their country, were led to the unequal conflict!

It was officially announced, and vehemently affirmed, that the sole object of the war was to subdue the Rebellion and maintain the Constitution, — the latter clause being popularly understood to include a guaranty of the perpetuity of slave-holding! The veteran retainers of the slave Barons, at the North, were willing to sustain the government, on the implied condition that the government should still sustain slavery; but they stipulated, tenaciously, that the war against the rebels should not become "an Abolition crusade." The loyal press, accurately reflecting the policy of the Administration, proclaimed to the world — as often as the world gave signs of being incredulous — that it was by no means the object of the war to abolish slavery, but simply to put down the Rebellion; although it was perfectly obvious, all the while, that, if the Rebellion were really subdued, the ulcer that emitted this virus of treason must be extracted from the body politic.

Whenever a man ventured to intimate, here and there, that this pretended distinction between the Rebellion and slavery was purely factitious, — like the attempt to discriminate between the hand that strikes you and the will that dictates the blow, — he was sharply reminded that this was exclusively a war for the Union, and that in maintaining the Union we upheld the "constitutional rights" of all the citizens, — the term "constitutional rights" being a delicate expression to indicate the supposed right of slave-holders to property in negroes!

But this illusive distinction, so irrational in theory, became absolutely pernicious in practice. Our generals, while ostensibly marching against the rebels, still paid fealty to the chief rebel by sending back fugitive slaves. GENERAL BUTLER in Maryland, and GENERAL MCCLELLAN in Virginia, took pains to assure the country that their espousal to the Union did not qualify the allegiance they owed to slavery.

But these gentlemen were not insensible to the admonition of events, and soon ceased to degrade their military functions to the service of the slaveholders; whereas General Kelley in Western Virginia, and General Halleck in Missouri, six months after the opening of the war, were still so far infatuated — if they were not misrepresented by the press — as to permit the flag of the Union to shelter the kidnapper. Such acts involve the highest moral treason to the cause of the Republic; they give virtual "aid and comfort" to the rebels, because they indicate sympathy for the odious system which is the spring and motive power of the insurrection. Wherever they have been committed, the cause of the Union has been weakened and scandalized; for if the cause of the Union be not the cause of liberty, in opposition to that chattel slavery which the Rebellion aims to perpetuate, in the name of God, why are we resisting the Rebellion?

But — the "constitutional rights" aforesaid? If the view of the Constitution which we have advocated in this essay be correct, that phrase cannot fairly be said to cover any right to property in men. But, admitting that it does, is it not enough to reply, that the Constitution contemplates no such crisis as this? that it were madness to preserve a Constitution at the price of sacrificing the nation to which it belongs? and that the dictates of self-preservation, among sane people, take precedence of technicalities? When your life is beset by robbers, is that man your friend who, instead of springing to your rescue and assailing the assassins with any weapon he can lay his hands upon, contents himself with getting up a certificate of your moral character, and proving that you merit fair treatment? No more is that government true to its country's real need when the life of the nation is beset, if it limit its efforts to the technicalities of a Constitution, and, so hampered, fail to deal upon the enemy an effective blow. Of what avail is it to sedulously shelter the Constitution, while the nation expires? Whereas if the nation be rescued, though by a violation of the Constitution, the emergency pleads for the technical illegality, and there is ample opportunity to restore the law. It is unlawful to inflict violence upon an unoffending man; yet, in an emergency which the law does not foresee, you may snatch him from fire or water by the hair of his head. All attempts to ustify the government in protecting slavery, by pleading supposed constitutional sanctions, amount to simple nonsense. If slavery had not forfeited whatever protection it was wont to claim under the Constitution, then no pirate ever forfeited his life to an outraged law.

IV.

THE PROGRAMME OF THE PRESIDENT, AND THE LESSON OF EVENTS.

THESE persistent attempts to shelter slavery, while affecting to destroy the Rebellion of which slavery is the soul, demonstrate the loathsome subserviency to which the Republic had bent. It is claimed that this unnatural policy of the Administration was the imperative requirement of public opinion in this country, and we do not feel authorized to doubt it; for the land had fallen into a superstition kindred to the worst debasement of heathenism; and, as the crocodile was sacred to the Egyptians, and the wolf to the Romans, slavery had become sacred to this nation. Whatever might suffer besides, slavery must be protected. To conspire against the Union was wicked; to propose the abolition of slavery was impious. On the scale of criminality, the rebels were *comparatively* guilty, the Abolitionists *superlatively* so!

But events qualify all programmes, — especially such as were arranged on the basis of expediency. When GENERAL BUTLER, at Fortress Monroe, found some hundreds of fugitives claiming the hospitality of the Republic, the voice of humanity and the dictates of common sense — backed by a seasonable admonition from Massachusetts — required a change of policy. Whether the fugitives were *men*, and therefore entitled to the protection of the army ostensibly enlisted for freedom, was a point which the judicious General blandly waived; but, men or *property*, nobody could deny that they were "CONTRABAND," — being claimed by rebel masters, — capable of being employed for the government or against it, and in that character might be safely sheltered by the American flag. The sympathetic response to this shrewd decision which came back to him from all the free States assured GENERAL BUTLER that the heart of the nation was ready to sanction whatever blows might be inflicted upon slavery, with due regard to the "constitutional rights" of the slave-masters.

Meantime, the army of the Potomac adhered to the original policy; and Congress, sitting in special session, seemed reluctant to implicate the Republic in any act of hostility to slavery.

On the eve of the ill-fated march upon Manassas, the following general order was issued from the Department of Washington: —

"HEADQUARTERS, DEPARTMENT OF WASHINGTON,
Washington, D. C., July 17, 1861.

"*General Orders*, No. 33.]

"Fugitive slaves will under no pretext whatever be permitted to reside, or be in any way harbored, in the quarters and camps of the troops serving in this Department. Neither will such slaves be allowed to accompany troops on the march. Commanders of troops will be held responsible for a strict observance of the order.

"By command of

BRIG.-GEN. MANSFIELD.

"THEO. TALBOT, *Assist. Adj.-General.*"

Now, among the fugitives thus officially excluded from the camp there were doubtless men whose sagacity, fidelity, and intimate knowledge of the country would have been of the highest service to the army, and who might, indeed, have averted from us, by seasonable information and warning, the havoc and shame of the dreadful defeat which followed. But our natural allies were repelled, contrary to every suggestion of common sense, and our army led blindfold, as it were, into the rebel trap, because the government preferred to peril its devoted volunteers to inflicting any damage upon slavery! Those who believe that God punishes the perverseness of nations by special judgments will be confirmed in their conviction by the example of the great calamity which fell upon the Republic so suddenly after its violation of the obvious dictates of justice and consistency.

In the providence of God the defeat at Manassas helped the country to a wiser appreciation of the strength of our enemy, and impressed upon the government the necessity of striking one blow at least where he is most vulnerable. "The proposition of emancipation which shook ancient Athens, followed close upon the disaster at Cheronæa; and the statesman who moved it afterwards vindicated himself by saying that it proceeded not from him, but from Cheronæa. The act of Congress punishing the rebels by giving freedom to their slaves *employed against us* — familiarly known as the Confiscation Act — passed the Senate on the morning after the disaster at Manassas." *

Who can doubt that a more tractable spirit — a wiser readiness to acknowledge the indications of the Divine will — might have averted from the country that calamitous chastisement? And if we owe the Confiscation Act to the salutary reverse at Manassas, we have to lament that the admonition administered by that defeat was soon forgotten. Only two days after the rout of our army, while Washington lay exposed to capture, and while volunteers were pouring from the free States to its defence, the Attorney-General wrote to the United States Marshal in Kansas, requiring him (much against his will) to return fugitive slaves to Missouri; and informing him that a neglect to execute the Fugitive Slave Bill would be regarded by the President as an "official misdemeanor." This characteristic act was followed up by the letter of the President, — dictated probably by the remonstrance of Mr. HOLT and others of the border States, — qualifying the proclamation of GENERAL

* Hon. Charles Sumner.

FREMONT, and thereby quenching the most genuine enthusiasm for the cause of the Union that had been inspired since the commencement of the war. The veil is yet to be removed from the counsels that procured the removal of the gallant Californian; but whenever the facts shall be made known, if they do not show that hostility to slavery cost him the favor of his government, and his command of the Western Department, the country will experience an agreeable surprise.

V.

MUST THE NATION DIE, THAT THE BARONS MAY WIELD THE WHIP?

THE course of the government appears yet more astonishing, when we consider how small a proportion of the American people have any pecuniary interest in the system for which these extraordinary sacrifices were made. The whole number of slave-holders, according to the last census, did not exceed four hundred thousand, out of whom it is estimated that not above one hundred thousand are largely interested in slave property.

And yet for the sake of this petty oligarchy the immediate welfare of thirty millions of people is put in jeopardy, besides the prospective welfare of all their posterity! The free States have sent into the camp, for the defence of the Republic, a host of volunteers outnumbering all the slave-masters, whether treasonable or loyal; and should not the life of every soldier who rallied to the Federal standard have been as dear to the government as the interest of a slave-holder? — even a slave-holder of a border State, characterized by the dubious loyalty that inclined him to serve the Union so long as the Union should serve slavery!

Where was the equity of requiring the twenty millions of people found in the loyal States to contribute their blood and their treasure to the support of a government, that perversely exposed itself to destruction, out of regard to the interest of a petty squad of slave-masters, most of whom were in arms for its overthrow?

We venture to affirm that so irritating an instance of perversity and infatuation, involving the peril of such incalculable interests, and so violent a series of paradoxes, is not to be found on the pages of history.

VI.

THE WAR DEGRADED IN THE INTEREST OF SLAVERY.

We have been often admonished, during the present eventful year, that the practical statesman cannot conform himself to the theory of the philosopher, or to the requirements of abstract justice. We promptly deny the proposition. At least, we insist that, so far as the theory of the philosopher is based upon the moral law, and elaborated in consonance with common sense, it dictates a course which the statesman will always find practicable and eminently safe.

There is no error of statesmen more common, or less excusable, than that of consciously violating the law of right, under the temptation of expediency. All our calamities as a nation have sprung from this propensity; here is the spring of all our political depravity; here sin entered, and death by sin; and it by no means confirms our trust in the wisdom of our present rulers, to hear them use the old plea of expediency as an excuse for neglecting justice. Can they flatter themselves that the Almighty, whose dark judgment eclipses the land, is to be any longer mocked by so lame a pretext for practical infidelity? If it be God who reigns, and not Satan, then a nation must expect deliverance in the path of justice and honesty, not in that of expediency and craft.

In the beginning, every intelligent and conscientious person in the North hailed the war as a great conflict of ideas, which was to mark an epoch in human affairs, and with which enlightened and humane men might sympathize the world over. "March at the head of the ideas of your age," said LOUIS NAPOLEON, "and then these ideas will follow and support you. If you march behind them, they will drag you on. And if you march against them, they will certainly prove your downfall." No man can question that a war of emancipation would marshal under the banner of the Union the most potent ideas that fire the present age, and a spirit that animates both the better part of the American people and all other civilized nations, — a *moral energy*, in fact, which the process of time and the culture of society must intensify and augment. "March at the head of the ideas of your age," had been the constant cry of wisdom to our rulers since the opening of this terrible controversy. But the government had degraded the war into a mere scramble of political rivalry, the sacrifices and miseries of which threatened to be indefinitely prolonged, besides being fruitless. The government had proclaimed decisively, by its unnatural policy hitherto, that there was no great PRINCIPLE at issue between the contending parties, — that, while the rebels were fighting for a Southern Confederacy *and* SLAVERY, the government was contending for the Union *and* SLAVERY. What could it matter to mankind whether the Confederacy or the Union prevailed, if slavery was to be cherished by both? Why should the country peril its bravest sons on the battle-field, and lavish hundreds of millions of treasure to sustain MR. LINCOLN against JEFFERSON DAVIS, if both were so ardently espoused to slavery as to make its interest paramount?

VII.

GOD'S ULTIMATUM.

The war had been waged during more than six months, before a change of policy began to be indicated at Washington. The loyal States had sent to the aid of the government an aggregate of seven hundred thousand men,* — one of the largest military forces that was ever enrolled. The immense army, reviving the image of an Asiatic host in the plenitude of Oriental empire, had been equipped, drilled, and sustained at an expense of a million and a half of money per day. Many of the noblest of our young men, in the generous effusion of patriotic enthusiasm, had laid down their lives to vindicate the Republic. The loyal millions in the free States had cheerfully submitted to taxation, to derangements of business, to social deprivations and domestic anxiety; and many of them had resigned with dignity their dearest hopes for the sake of restoring the integrity of the Union. Was not the government obligated to do everything in its power, to use every instrumentality sanctioned by the usages of war, to attack its haughty enemy

* Report of the Secretary of War, December, 1861.

at every vulnerable point, with a view to bringing the war to a speedy and auspicious termination? Yet, up to that time, it had, with a prodigal waste of opportunity, not only refused to employ free colored men and Indians in its service, — although the rebels had turned upon our Western border both Indians and convicts, while they had regiments of negroes under martial drill, — but it had obstinately repelled four millions of allies, because they could not be welcomed without overthrowing slavery!

Hence, with all the resources at command of the government, with all the loyalty and generosity of the nation, the cause of the Union still stood on the defensive, and the great struggle seemed to stretch into the future, an interminable prospect of carnage and disaster. The Rebellion stood unharmed, its vaunting spirit unrebuked, its diabolic propensities unchecked; because slavery was the substance of it, and the government had not felt authorized to harm slavery!

Secure in the trust that the power of the Union would not be turned against slavery, the South boasted that the piratical system was "a tower of strength" to the rebel cause. It was estimated that the secure possession of the slave population would enable the rebels to place six hundred thousand men in the field; and that, in spite of the numerical superiority of the North, the South would sustain the practical supremacy, since it was capable of sending to the camp all its able-bodied freemen, without weakening the industrial force that must provide the means of subsistence. The following testimony from a Southern journal shows how this advantage was appreciated: —

"THE SLAVES AS A MILITARY ELEMENT IN THE SOUTH. — The total white population of the eleven States now comprising the Confederacy is 6,000,000, and therefore, to fill up the ranks of the proposed army (600,000), about ten per cent of the entire white population will be required. In any other country than our own such a draft could not be met; but the Southern States can furnish that number of men, and still not leave the material interests of the country in a suffering condition. Those who are incapacitated for bearing arms can oversee the plantations, and *the negroes can go on undisturbed in their usual labors.* In the North the case is different; the men who join the army of subjugation are the laborers, the producers, and the factory operatives. Nearly every man from that section, especially those from the rural districts, leaves some branch of industry to suffer during his absence. *The institution of slavery in the South alone enables her to place in the field a force much larger in proportion to her white population than the North*, or indeed any country which is dependent entirely on free labor. The institution is a tower of strength to the South, *particularly at the present crisis*, and our enemies will be likely to find that the 'moral cancer,' about which their orators are so fond of prating, is really *one* *of the most effective weapons employed against the Union by the South.* Whatever number of men may be needed for this war, we are confident our people stand ready to furnish. We are all enlisted for the war, and there must be no holding back until the independence of the South is fully acknowledged." *

Thus Providence still adhered to the terms in which the case had been stated at the opening of the war: You shall not overcome the Rebellion except you abolish slavery. You shall choose between liberty and the Union, on one hand, and slavery and anarchy, on the other. If you persist in maintaining slavery, then no more Union; for JUDGMENT WILL I LAY TO THE LINE, AND RIGHTEOUSNESS TO THE PLUMMET; AND YOUR COVENANT WITH DEATH SHALL BE DISANNULLED, AND YOUR AGREEMENT WITH HELL SHALL NOT STAND.

That this was God's ultimatum, no man who recognized a Divine Providence in human affairs could longer doubt. Would the government accept salvation on these righteous conditions, or would it persist in following the illusive dictates of expediency, and so founder in the storm?

* Mobile (Ala.) Advertiser.

VIII.

A NEW POLICY IMPERATIVE.

It was consistent neither with the nature of man nor with the instincts implanted in the Republic permanently to endure so irrational a policy. The moral sense of the best men and the reason of the most thoughtful were alike shocked by the odiously false position which the loyal part of the nation was thus made to occupy.

The convictions of the better part of our people began to find expression, just previous to the meeting of the present Congress, in the eloquent remonstrances of men like the Hon. Gerrit Smith and Senator Sumner, and in the changed tone of members of the Cabinet and officers of the army. "Nobody can deny," said Mr. Sumner, "that slavery is the ruling idea of this rebellion. It is slavery that marshals these hosts, and breathes into their embattled ranks its own barbarous fire. It is slavery which stamps its character alike upon officers and men. It is slavery which inspires all, from the general to the trumpeter. It is slavery which speaks in the word of command, and which sounds in the morning drum-beat. It is slavery which digs trenches and builds hostile forts. It is slavery which pitches its white tents and stations its sentries over against the national Capitol. It is slavery which sharpens the bayonet and casts the bullet; which points the cannon and scatters the shell, blazing, bursting with death. Wherever this rebellion shows itself, — whatever form it takes, — whatever thing it does, — whatever it meditates, — it is moved by slavery; nay, it is slavery itself, incarnate, living, acting, raging, robbing, murdering, according to the essential law of its being."

Slavery may be seen also "in what it has inflicted upon us. There is not a community, — not a family, — not an individual, man, woman, or child, — who does not feel its heavy, bloody hand. Why these mustering armies? Why this drum-beat in your peaceful streets? Why these gathering means of war? Why these swelling taxes? Why these unprecedented loans? Why this derangement of business? Why among us the suspension of the *habeas corpus*, and the prostration of all safeguards of freedom? Why this constant solicitude visible in all your faces? The answer is clear. Slavery is the author, — the agent, — the cause. The anxious hours that you pass are darkened by slavery. The *habeas corpus* and all those safeguards of freedom which you adore have been prostrated by slavery. The business which you have lost has been filched by slavery. The millions of money now amassed by patriotic offerings are all snatched by slavery. The taxes now wrung out of your diminished means are all consumed by slavery. . . . . Does any community mourn gallant men, who, going forth joyous and proud beneath their country's flag, have been brought home cold and stiff, with its folds wrapped about them for a shroud? Let all who truly mourn the dead be aroused against slavery. Does a mother drop tears for a son, in the flower of his days cut down upon the distant battle-field, which he moistens with his youthful, generous blood? Let her know that slavery dealt the deadly blow, which took at once his life and her peace.

"You have seen slavery at all times militant whenever any proposition was brought forward with regard to it, and more than once threatening a dissolution of the Union. You have seen slavery for many years the animating principle of a conspiracy against the Union, while it matured its flagitious plans and obtained the mastery of Cabinet and President. And when the conspiracy had wickedly ripened, you have seen that it was only by concessions to slavery that it was encountered, as by similar concessions it had from the beginning been encouraged. You now see rebellion everywhere throughout the slave States elevating its bloody crest and threatening the existence of the national government, and all in the name of slavery, while it proposes to establish a new government whose corner-stone shall be slavery. Against this rebellion we wage war. It is our determination, as it is our duty, to crush it; and this will be done. The region now contested by the rebels belongs to the United States by every tie of government and of right. Some of it has been bought by our money, while all of it — with its rivers, harbors, and extensive coast — has become essential to our business in peace and to our defence in war. Union is a geographical, economical, commercial, political, military, and, if I may so say, even a fluvial necessity. Without union, peace on this continent is impossible; but life without peace is impossible also. Only by crushing this rebellion can union and peace be restored. Let this be seen in its reality, and who can hesitate? If this were done instantly, without further contest, then, besides all the countless advantages of every kind obtained by such restoration, two especial goods will be accomplished, — one political, and the other moral as well as political. First, the pretended right of Secession, with the whole pestilent extravagance of State sovereignty, which has supplied the machinery for this rebellion, and afforded a delusive cover for treason, will be trampled out, never again to disturb the majestic unity of the Republic. And, secondly, the unrighteous attempt to organize a new Confederacy solely for the sake of slavery, and with slavery as its cornerstone, will be overthrown. These two pretensions — one so shocking to our reason and the other so shocking to our moral nature — will disappear forever. And with their disappearance will commence a new epoch, the beginning of a grander period. But if by any accident the rebellion should prevail, then just in proportion to its triumph, whether through concession on our part or through successful force on the other part, will the Union be impaired and peace be impossible. Therefore, in the name of the Union, and for the sake of peace, are you summoned to the work. But how shall the rebellion be crushed? That is the question. Men, money, munitions of war, a well-supplied commissariat, means of transportation, — all these you have in abundance, in some particulars beyond the rebels. You have, too, the consciousness of a good cause, which in itself is an army. And yet thus far — until within a few days — the advantage has not been on our side. The explanation is easy. The rebels are combating at home, on their own soil, strengthened and maddened by slavery, which is to them an ally and a fanaticism. More thoroughly aroused than ourselves, — more terribly in earnest, — with every sinew strained to the utmost, — they freely use all the resources that God and nature put into their hands, raising against us not only the whole white population, but enlisting the war-whoop of the Indians, — cruising upon the sea in pirate ships to despoil our commerce, and at one swoop confiscating our property to the extent of hundreds of millions of dollars, while all this time their four millions of slaves, undisturbed at home, are freely contributing by their labor to sustain the war, which without them must soon expire.

"It remains for us to encounter the rebellion calmly and surely by a force superior to its own. But to this end something more will be needed than men or money. Our battalions must be reinforced by ideas, and we must strike directly at the origin and mainspring of the rebellion. I do not say now in what way or to what extent; but simply that we must strike; it may be by the system of a Massachusetts general, — BUTLER; it may be by that of FREMONT; or it may be by the grander system of JOHN QUINCY ADAMS. Reason and sentiment both concur in this policy, which is only according to the most common principles of human conduct. In no way can we do so much at so little cost. To the enemy such a blow will be a terror, to good men it will be an encouragement, and to foreign nations watching this contest it will be an earnest of something beyond a mere carnival of battle. There has been the cry, 'On to Richmond!' and still another worse cry, 'On to England!' Better than either is the cry, 'On to Freedom!' Let this be heard in the voices of your soldiers, — ay, let it resound in the purposes of the government, — and victory must be ours. By this sign conquer. . . . . . That men should still hesitate to strike at slavery, is only another illustration of human weakness. The English Republicans, in their bloody contest with the crown, hesitated for a long time to fire upon the king; but under the valiant lead of CROMWELL, surrounded by his well-trained Ironsides, they banished all such scruple, and you know well the result. The king was not shot, but his head was brought to the block.

"The duty which I suggest, if not urgent now, as *a military necessity in just self-defence*, will present itself constantly, on other grounds, *as our armies advance in the slave States or land on their coasts.* If it does not stare us in the face at this moment, it is because unhappily we are still everywhere on the defensive. As we begin to be successful, it must rise before us for practical decision; and you cannot avoid it. There will be slaves in your camps, or within your extended lines, whose condition you must determine. There will be slaves also claimed by rebels, whose continued chattelhood you will scorn to recognize. The decision of these two cases will settle the whole great question. Nor can the rebels complain. They challenge our armies to enter upon their territory in the free exercise of all the powers of war, — according to which, as you well know, all private interests are subordinated to the public safety, which for the time becomes the supreme law above all other laws, and above the Constitution itself. If everywhere under the flag of the Union, — in its triumphant march, — freedom is substituted for slavery, this outrageous rebellion will not be the first instance in history where God has turned the wickedness of man into a blessing; nor will the example of Samson stand alone when

10

he gathered honey out of the carcass of the dead and rotten lion. . . . . .

"Thank God! our government is strong; but thus far all signs denote that it is not strong enough to save the Union and at the same time to save slavery. One or the other must suffer, and just in proportion as you reach forth to protect slavery, do you protect this accursed rebellion; nay, you give to it that aid and comfort which, under our Constitution, is treason itself. Perversely and pitifully do you postpone that sure period of reconciliation, not only between the two sections, — not only between the men of the North and the men of the South, — but, more beautiful still, between the slave and his master, without which that true tranquillity which we all seek cannot be permanently assured to our country. Believe it; only through such reconciliation, under the sanction of freedom, can you remove all occasion of contention hereafter; only in this way can you cut off the head of this great rebellion, and at the same time extirpate that principle of evil, which, if allowed to remain, must shoot forth in perpetual discord, if not in other rebellions; only in this way can you command that safe victory — without which this contest will be vain — which will have among its conquests indemnity for the past and security for the future, — the noblest indemnity and the strongest security ever won, because founded in the redemption of a race. . . . . .

"There is a classical story of a mighty hunter whose life in the Book of Fate had been made to depend upon the preservation of a brand which was burning at his birth. The brand, so full of destiny, was snatched from the flames and carefully preserved by his prudent mother. Meanwhile the hunter became powerful and invulnerable to mortal weapons. But at length the mother, indignant at his cruelty to her own family, flung the brand upon the flames, and the hunter died. The story of that hunter, so powerful and invulnerable to mortal weapons, is now repeated in this rebellion, and slavery is the fatal brand. Let our government, which has thus far preserved slavery with maternal care, simply fling it upon the flames which itself has madly aroused, and the rebellion will die at once." *

* Sumner's Address at Cooper Institute, November 27, 1861.

IX.

PROVIDENTIAL DOOM OF THE BARONS.

THE morning of Tuesday, October 29th, 1861, dawned upon the most imposing spectacle that has illustrated the naval history of this continent. The great expedition — the Armada of our annals — lifted its anchors at Hampton Roads, and sailed toward the Gulf, to meet its unknown destiny. For weeks its destination had been the theme of speculation, its success the object of national solicitude. From the first the magnitude of the enterprise and the mystery that clothed its vast proportions had inspired the nation with the confident assurance that it was to open a new act in the tragedy of the Rebellion, and give a permanent ascendency to the cause of the Union.

The great expedition swept majestically away in the splendor of that auspicious morning, and vanished down the Southern coast. The prayers and hopes of a loyal people went onward with the fleet as it traversed those hostile waters. Well might prayers ascend, and well might hope abound over fear; for when the signal gun was fired that morning from the *Wabash*, and the proud flag-ship moved out between the capes, she bore the ark of a new covenant, the seal of a new civil dispensation. For the earnest of success, the pledge of victory, was not alone in that imposing line of battle-ships, with its mighty armament of stern men, and its frowning batteries gorged with cannon, shot, and shell, but also — and may we not say pre-eminently? — in certain instructions from the War Department charged with the seeds of liberty. These are the words addressed to the commanding general: —

"You will, however, in general avail yourself of the services of any persons, whether fugitives from labor or not, who may offer them to the national government; you will employ such persons in such services as they may be fitted for, either as ordinary employees, or, if special circumstances seem to require it, in any other capacity, with such organization, in squads, companies, or otherwise, as you deem most beneficial to the service. This, however, not to mean a general arming of them for military service. You will assure all loyal masters that Congress will provide just compensation to them for the loss of the services of the persons so employed."

These words contain the germ of a NEW POLICY, for they are understood to have received the deliberate sanction of the President, as well as of the Secretary of War. They are confirmed by the sentiments more recently expressed in the Reports of the Secretary of War and the Secretary of the Navy. They mark an entire revolution in the policy of the Federal Government. Slavery is no longer to be protected. It is to take its due place among mundane interests — of the baser sort. It is to be abandoned to the chances of the war which it has had the temerity to kindle. Having invoked a shower of stones, it must abide, in its own glass house, the natural consequences. GENERAL LANE, of Kansas, had expressed the popular feeling when he said that it was the duty of the government "to put down rebellion, and let slavery take care of itself." The Administration has at length acquiesced in the popular decision; and the great expedition has launched the new policy upon South Carolina.

The instructions to GENERAL SHERMAN, though lacking the positive form of a proclamation of emancipation, contain most of the elements of such a paper. "First, martial law is hereby declared; for the powers committed to the discretion of the General are derived from that law, and not from the late Confiscation Act of Congress. Secondly, fugitive slaves are not to be surrendered. Thirdly, all coming within the camp are to be treated as freemen. Fourthly, they may be employed in such service as they may be fitted for. Fifthly, in squads, companies, or otherwise, with the single limitation that this is not to mean 'a *general* arming of them for military service.' And, sixthly, compensation, through Congress, is promised to loyal masters, — saying nothing of rebel masters. All this is a little short of a proclamation of emancipation, — not unlike that of old CAIUS MARIUS, when he landed on the coast of Etruria, and, according to PLUTARCH, proclaimed liberty to the slaves."

The policy here foreshadowed — confirmed as it has recently been by the President in his Message, by the Reports of the Secretaries of the War Department and the Navy, and by the obvious temper of the Congress now in session — proclaims the doom of slavery on the American continent. Nothing, we are confident, can arrest the retribution which has been preparing for so many years, which so many wrongs have tended to provoke, and which is demanded alike by the justice of God, the development of civilization, and the aspiration of every noble heart in every clime of the globe.

The development of the slave-holding despotism has borne such fruit as no man foresaw who consented to tolerate its growth. The effects of the system have been so palpably *retributive*, as to evince a Divine agency working out its destruction, if not the destruction of those leagued with it. We are too much in the habit of estimating the evils of slavery with exclusive reference to the Negro race. Its direct and obvious effects upon the slaves themselves are doubtless revolting enough; but the most terrific effects of the system appear, not in its results to the Negro, but in its results to the white man. Slavery may not be an *obvious* injury to every individual slave; but we maintain that it *is* an obvious injury to every individual master,—to every free family,—to every State,—and to the very LIFE of the Republic. Forty years ago, actuated by commercial selfishness and by our antipathies to the African race, we supposed that the perpetuity of slavery would damage nobody but the helpless negro. But behold how God has punished our cruelty, and confounded our expectations! The African race in America has passed through a baptism of fire; but it has multiplied as the Israelites did under the oppressions of Egypt. It has become a more civilized and mighty race, drawing from its taskmasters more mental vigor and greater relish for freedom, from year to year, till it has become a terror in the land, no longer to be trusted, hardly to be restrained.

While God has thus been strengthening the servile race, he has been weakening their oppressors. While the Negro has been rising toward civilization, the white man of the South has been sinking into barbarism. Ignorance and superstition, cruelty and vice, violence and anarchy, reign paramount in the slave-holding States. There never was seen such a sudden and wholesale relapse of great communities into hopeless barbarism. The records of the social life of those States have been, for some years, like pages gathered from the annals of the tenth century. Such violent despotism over private judgment,— such sanguinary sway of Lynch-law, — such subjugation of cities to brutal mobs, and of States to revolutionary anarchy, — such swaggering pretensions to "honor" and "chivalry," united with crimes that only the hangman can properly punish, — such spectacles, which make up the every-day life of the South, almost persuade a man that he is reading a chronicle of the Middle Ages, and not an American newspaper reporting contemporaneous events.

As little did we foresee the effect of slavery on the safety and integrity of the American government. When it clamored for protection, we never thought it would aspire to rule. When it aspired to rule, we never thought it would *conspire* to ruin the Republic if it were voted out of power. But such is the nature of the system, that it makes everything it touches *subservient;* and, soon as it comes to be resisted, breaks every treaty, defies every consequence, and malignantly stabs the nation that has warmed it into power. Itself based upon injustice, rapine, and cruelty, it is not conciliated by fair play, restrained by considerations of social well-being, or affected by the prospect of boundless carnage. It is a creature of lust, aggression, and violence, and its legitimate influence is always fatal just in proportion to its power and opportunity.

With the nature and tendencies of slavery so clearly disclosed as they now are in the state of Southern society, and in this most wicked rebellion, if there is an American freeman who can apologize for it any longer, it must be a case of infatuation utterly without parallel. And if this bloody quarrel, which slavery has ruthlessly provoked, is ever settled without rooting the deadly curse out of the land, we shall bequeath a new quarrel to our children, and untold calamities to mankind.

We were willing to tolerate slavery from a fallacious sense of constitutional obligation; and we would even violate conscience to keep the faith our fathers were believed to have bound us by. But since slavery was not content with being tolerated, but insisted on being our dictator, — since *she will be our autocrat or our destroyer*, — and since she has taken down the sword and summoned us to mortal combat, — away with all forbearance, and all compromise, and let the wicked harlot die. She has released us from the old compact, *whatever that may have involved;* and God be thanked for the madness of despotism, that has broken the dangerous bond! She has exasperated every freeman by seventy years of insolence, — by seventy years of broken faith and culminating crimes, — and now, by the just God in heaven, and by the holy instincts of freedom, let her perish by the sword she has compelled us to draw!

We have endured everything from slavery that human nature can endure, because our temper is forbearing, our manners are pacific, and our pursuits compatible only with peace. We have consented to be a reproach to civilized nations, because of our complicity in this great wrong. We have consented to bear more than our just proportion of the burdens of government, and have received less than our just share of its emoluments. We have submitted to have our citizens mobbed, imprisoned, and hung, for no crime but that of being born in a free State, and loving their natural birthright. We have endured insults and aggressions, fraud and violence, in the halls of Congress, and in our own free cities. We have given up the weak to the fangs of the slave-hunter, and seen the mark of the beast set upon the forehead of our most illustrious men. All this has not been enough. Slavery has demanded more; and when we refused to grant more, she seized her wicked bludgeon, and tried to demolish the fabric of that fair Union which had sheltered her treasonable head. Now let her have what she has invoked. Let it be war to the death. Let the monstrous aggressor find no shelter, henceforth, under the flag she has profaned and betrayed.

We compassionate the Southern people, so hopelessly involved in the swift-footed vengeance that must sweep their land. They are not radically more guilty than ourselves; only the diabolical system that has possessed them so long has *inoculated* many of them with its own malignity. We feel like making great allowance for the bad schooling those people have suffered from. So deplorably has slavery enervated their moral principles and darkened their sense of right, that they no longer realize either what they do or what they are. They are the saddest victims of their own oppression. They are like drunkards besotted by their cups, and madly clinging to the terrible vice that has ruined them. O, for *their* sake, — even more than for our own, — let us swear eternal hostility to the system that has perverted a noble people, and turned a fruitful land into a howling desert! True, we must bear the sword against them, — for their salvation and ours we must still appeal to the God of battles, — but, as Heaven is our witness, compassion shall temper the warfare they have provoked; and our vengeance fall only upon that villanous despotism which has brought discord between us, and upon those who deliriously espouse its fate.

Nor need we fear that a war of emancipation and subjugation — (for this war must involve the subjugation, if not *extirpation*, of the Southern Barons) — will permanently alienate the rebellious States from the Union. Such apprehensions are refuted by the experience of other nations. There are few wounds inflicted by the sword upon the transitory sentiments of races, which time does not benignantly heal; and a quarrel, fought out with lusty vigor, often ends in cordial friendship. All this has been repeatedly proved, from the days of the Roman empire downward; and in no country more plainly than in Great Britain, where the most virulent civil wars have left no darker memento than a few suits of battered armor laid up at Westminster, or a broken image on some cathedral shrine.

A weak and vacillating war, *irritating* without *subduing* the South, and leaving the root of its antipathy undisturbed, would perpetuate our animosities, and sow the seeds of interminable conflicts. But a vigorous and resolute war, with a regenerating principle at its base, with justice on its banner, with universal freedom for its aim, will renew and conciliate the South, while it vindicates the integrity of the nation.

"The sword! — a name of dread; yet when
Upon the freeman's thigh 't is bound, —
While for his altar and his hearth,
While for the land that gave him birth,
The war-drums roll, the trumpets sound, —
How sacred is it then!
Whenever for the truth and right
It flashes in the van of fight, —
Whether in some wild mountain pass,
As that where fell Leonidas;
Or on some sterile plain and stern, —
A Marston or a Bannockburn;
Or 'mid fierce crags and bursting rills, —
The Switzer's Alps, gray Tyrol's hills;
Or, as when sunk the Armada's pride,
It gleams above the stormy tide;
Still, still, whene'er the battle's word
Is Liberty, — when men do stand
For Justice and their native land, —
Then Heaven bless the sword!"

The rebel States are like fields overgrown with briers, and infested by beasts of prey. It requires the stern husbandry of war to clear away the excrescences, to expel the brutal occupants, and restore those lands to the uses of civilization. There is a wild crop of ignorance, and a depraved herd of desperadoes, cumbering and infesting those States, that require to be turned under by the ploughshare of battle, or driven out by the besom of judgment. The cause of civilization cannot be longer retarded by the oligarchy of Slave Barons, who have sinned so deeply against the light of the age, and conspired so perfidiously against the glory of their country. Having repudiated the better attributes of humanity, and impeded Christian development on the continent, they have forfeited the immunities of humanity, and made the world their foe. They fall under the Divine law that exposes the nettle to the hoe, and the wolf to the rifle; for the law of Providence is, that noxious and ravenous things shall perish whenever the expansion of society requires a new field, and the growth of noble men a wider career.

Let the providential work of renovation go forward in the track of an army conscious of its high mission, and dignified by the majesty of great ideas, till violence shall no more be heard in the land, nor wasting nor destruction within its borders; till the myrtle shall supplant the brier, and the rose adorn the desert; and the South will rise up, clothed in her right mind, and bless the Federal sword that flashed God's righteous judgment upon the haughty and cruel; while gentler hands build up the bulwarks of society anew, for a perpetual habitation of Honor and Freedom, of Peace and of Glory.

X.

THESEUS AND THE MINOTAUR. — LESSON OF THE EPOCH.

THERE is a Greek story of MINOS, the magnificent king of Crete, who exacted of the Athenians an annual tribute of seven youths and seven maidens, whom he sacrificed to the MINOTAUR, a horrible monster having the body of a man, the head of a bull, and the teeth of a lion. Every year, at the approach of the spring equinox, came a herald from Crete to demand this tribute; and the devoted victims were borne away in a black-sailed ship, amid the lamentations of the people. But when THESEUS, the young hero, came to Athens, and saw the beautiful youths and maidens being selected by lot for the odious sacrifice, and witnessed the shame of their king, his father, and the sorrow of the city, he generously cast his fate with the destined victims, slew the Minotaur, and released the land from that dreadful scourge.

The Greek legend finds an impressive application in republican America. The king of the South, whose name is Cotton, has levied tribute upon the nation for many sorrowful years. He has claimed our fairest and holiest, — our honor, our freedom, and our religion. In the black-sailed, evil-boding ship of compromise we have sent them to the tyrant, and he has cast them into the den of the Minotaur, the monster man-beast, slavery. But God has sent us deliverance in the guise of calamity. The war is our THESEUS, which, girded by the martial strength of the North, and gloriously apparelled in the panoply of freedom, goes forth to slay the Minotaur, and release the land forever from tyranny and trouble.

Could this humble book gain the ear of a single man sitting in the Capitol, it would say: —

No longer offend justice or mock our woe by affecting to wed the INCOMPATIBLE.

Slavery and freedom can never be married so long as hell is alien to heaven. Their characters and tendencies, their aims and desires, are completely hostile. Slave society rests upon robbery, — for it holds by force what it has no claim to hold in equity, — asserting that claim of property in man which is repugnant to natural justice; free society rests upon the voluntary industry of the people, and is guarded by equity. Slave society tyrannizes over the weak; free society extends over the weak the protection of law. Slave society makes brute force supreme; free society makes justice supreme. In slave society a handful of aristocrats govern the State, and the masses of the inhabitants are disregarded like cattle; in free society, political power is distributed among all the people, and the most vigorous thinker is the mightiest man. In slave society, everything is at the mercy of an unthinking and capricious despotism, and the tendency of the community is irretrievably downward; but in free society great questions are settled by discussion, by reflection, by reason, — every man's interest is safe, because natural justice is revered, and everything is open to investigation, and so the community is continually being elevated, and fortified by the private conscience and public intelligence.

Such are the two hostile interests that have been subsisting in this Republic, from the beginning. Our fathers, with many scruples and doubts, set them up housekeeping, in the same edifice, because they supposed that slave society would soon die a natural death, and they were scarcely prepared to kill it by violent means. For seventy years these two types of society have been developing in the nation, — each according to its nature, each obedient to its own instinct. In the exact ratio of their growth has been their aggression upon each other. When the house began to resound with their strife, all the peace-makers turned out to settle the quarrel. The more they tried to settle it, the more fiercely the quarrel raged; and, step by step, by a series of ineffectual compromises that only irritated what they were expected to heal, we have journeyed on to civil war.

Suppose you plant Canada thistles on one side of your garden, and a bed of strawberry plants on the opposite side, and charge them not to meddle with each other! You will soon find that they *will* meddle with each other,—not because they are wilful, but because each must obey the law of its own nature. Now slave society and free society have their peculiar instincts, and *each develops agreeably to its own law.* THEY MUST ENCROACH UPON EACH OTHER; THEY MUST CONFLICT; THEY MUST QUARREL;—and what God and Nature have thus made hostile we cannot join together in harmony. Slave society imbues those who grow up under its spirit with a despotic and lawless disposition. Free society imbues people with a sense of justice, liberalizes and elevates the mind, and prepares the heart to feel the liveliest sympathy for the weak and the oppressed. Thus, the tendencies of the two systems, by their legitimate operation, involve collision and strife. How can we help ourselves? Can the man who was nourished at the breast of despotism be otherwise than tyrannical? Can the offspring of liberty disown his mother, or resist the generous impulses that spring from his blood? We must all have noticed how vain it is to attempt to override or suppress AN HEREDITARY TRAIT; and these *instincts* that are born with us, and fostered by the society in which we are reared, CANNOT BE CONTROLLED BY ANY ARBITRARY EDICT. We may as well make up our minds to face the fact, first as last: There will be no peace — at best, only a short *truce* — WHILE THESE BELLIGERENTS OCCUPY THE SAME HOUSE. May we not have a public opinion in America that shall recognize this fact without longer delay?

We have all railed, more or less, at the ultra men of the South; but we might as well rail at the Canada thistles when they manifest a desire to monopolize the garden. They are obeying the instincts of slave society, and our entreaties and expostulations — as the event has repeatedly proved — might as well have been addressed to thistles as to that class of men.

Suppose a company of Indian Thugs come into the neighborhood, buy a certain amount of real estate, and settle among us. It is the profession of the Thug to murder, and in him the tendency to murder has the force of an instinct. Murders are perpetrated, the community is in arms, and the Thugs are disposed of agreeably to law and equity. But, however heinous the crime, it was no greater than was to have been expected, in view of the habits of the Thugs. So with slave society. All its habitudes and instincts are aggressive and destructive. We are not denying that individual slave-holders may be very fair men. Some natures are proof against the worst social influences. We speak of the system of slavery in its essence and general effects. And we say that the most odious developments of Southern society are the legitimate outgrowths of slavery, — things which it is idle to protest against so long as we foster the seed that produces them.

We have complained, also, against the ultra anti-slavery men. But, candidly and philosophically viewed, what have *they* done but *obey the instincts of free society?* It was just as natural for free society to develop the Abolitionist party, as it was for your strawberry bed to throw out "runners" toward the Canada thistles. How futile it is to quarrel with any settled tendency of nature! How unwise it is to ignore such facts, instead of accommodating ourselves to them! We might as reasonably attempt to resist gravitation, or any other natural law, as attempt to carry out a peace policy in violation of these immutable conditions. Free society fills every bosom that is open to its influences with the love of free institutions, — with the love of justice, mercy, and manhood; and it inspires us, at the same time, with an irrepressible abhorrence of the injustice, the profligacy, and the ignorance which are the fruits of slavery. Under this influence, it is impossible that men should hold their peace. The full heart *will* make its emotions audible in burning words. Almost involuntarily — almost against a man's will — he thunders out his hatred of tyranny, and chants the hymns of Freedom. It is the Holy Spirit of God that impels his utterance, and timidity and compromise have no padlocks strong enough to shut the mouth of a live man, when the trumpet sounds and the hour has come.

Consider how obvious it is, as a general fact, that, when a conflict takes place in society between the good elements and the bad, there can be no permanent peace until the bad elements are eradicated. A bad principle in the social system is like a disease in the human system, — it is a source of irritation and unrest to the whole body politic. The patient is in ceaseless pain, apprehension, and depression; and even when he affects to rest, he moans, and tosses his limbs about, and starts as from ghastly dreams. How will you restore the man to his natural tranquillity, and to the enjoyment of his existence? Will you sit at his bed, and sing a lullaby? Will you expatiate on the blessings of rest? Will you remind him how commendable it is to be quiet and serene? Or will you endeavor *to expel the man's disease*, AND INSURE HIM TRANQUILLITY BY FIRST ENDOWING HIM WITH HEALTH?

That patient is our country. If you would not mock the misery of a man by affecting to lull him to rest while his malady rendered rest impossible, why will you mock the agony of our country, by singing lullabys, and ignoring the distemper that brings all the pain? American society has always had in its blood one virulent distemper. That distemper has been the source of all our trouble, agitation, discord, and danger; and now it has assumed an alarming phase. It has broken out in the ghastly form of TREASON. Now, what does the crisis require, at the hands of reasonable and faithful men? What can it require, but the RADICAL CURE OF THE PATIENT? Purify the social system, and the American Republic will have peace. This is the inflexible logic of the hour; will *they* heed it, to whom God has confided the solemn issues of the contest.

The great lesson which this eventful epoch is to teach our people, is devotion to liberty, and hatred of every influence that would qualify the principle or abridge the blessing. As our spiritual life has its fountain in Christ, and as the Church derives all its vitality from the Divine Spirit, so our political life has its spring in liberty, and the strength of the Republic lives in the spontaneous enthusiasm of free men.

Liberty, then, as the inalienable right of every man, of every race, as the spring of perpetuity and the crown of glory in the State, should be the song and joy of the nation, marching to battle, or exulting in victory. Through all the ages to come, it should usher the citizen to the post of duty in peaceful days, and fire him with antique heroism in the hour of danger. Mothers, with loyal fingers, should sprinkle their children in its name. Fair brides should be wedded to the peal of its auspicious bells. Old men, while reviving the pageantry of youth, should rehearse its inspiring story. Statues should rise to its honor in every village. Banners should blazon its conquests. Literature should embalm its fame, in the majestic march of historical periods, and in the splendor of epic verse. And Religion — beholding in Liberty her own co-worker — should invest it with spiritual sanctions, and awe the hearts of men before it with all the terrors of a righteous Providence.

DECEMBER 25, 1861.

Cambridge: Stereotyped and Printed by Welch, Bigelow, & Co.

www.ingramcontent.com/pod-product-compliance
Lightning Source LLC
LaVergne TN
LVHW050515100826
845148LV00002B/337